IMAGINATION IS
THE BEGINNING
OF CREATION.
YOU IMAGINE
WHAT YOU
DESIRE, YOU
WILL WHAT YOU
IMAGINE, AND
AT LAST, YOU
CREATE WHAT
YOU WILL.

– George Bernard Shaw

DREAMS · DESIRE · DESIGN

The Custom Home

Vernon D. Swaback, FAIA

"Desire–the qualities of the not yet said and the not yet made–is the reason for living. It is the core of the expressive instinct and must never by stymied."

– Louis Kahn

First published in Australia in 2001 by
The Images Publishing Group Pty Ltd
ACN 059 734 431
6 Bastow Place, Mulgrave, Victoria 3170, Australia
Telephone +613 9561 5544 Facsimile +613 9561 4860
email: books@images.com.au
www.imagespublishing.com.au

Printing rights: Copyright © The Images Publishing Group Pty Ltd, 2001
Contents: Copyright © 2001 Vernon D. Swaback, FAIA
The Images Publishing Group Reference Number: 478

ISBN 1 876907 40 1

Designed by Studio V Graphics
Production by The Graphic Image Studio Pty Ltd, Melbourne, Australia

Film by Mission Productions Ltd., Hong Kong
Printed by Everbest Printing Co. Ltd., Hong Kong

"Architecture is traditionally
an art form of the rich,
but it is also a medium that,
since prehistoric times,
has been used
to stake a place
for spiritual values
in every day life."

-Herbert Muschamp

"A house is a machine

for living."

– Le Corbusier

◆

"True, but the idea of

architecture

starts where that

thought leaves off."

– Frank Lloyd Wright

◆

"Doing a house

is so much harder than

doing a skyscraper."

– Philip Johnson

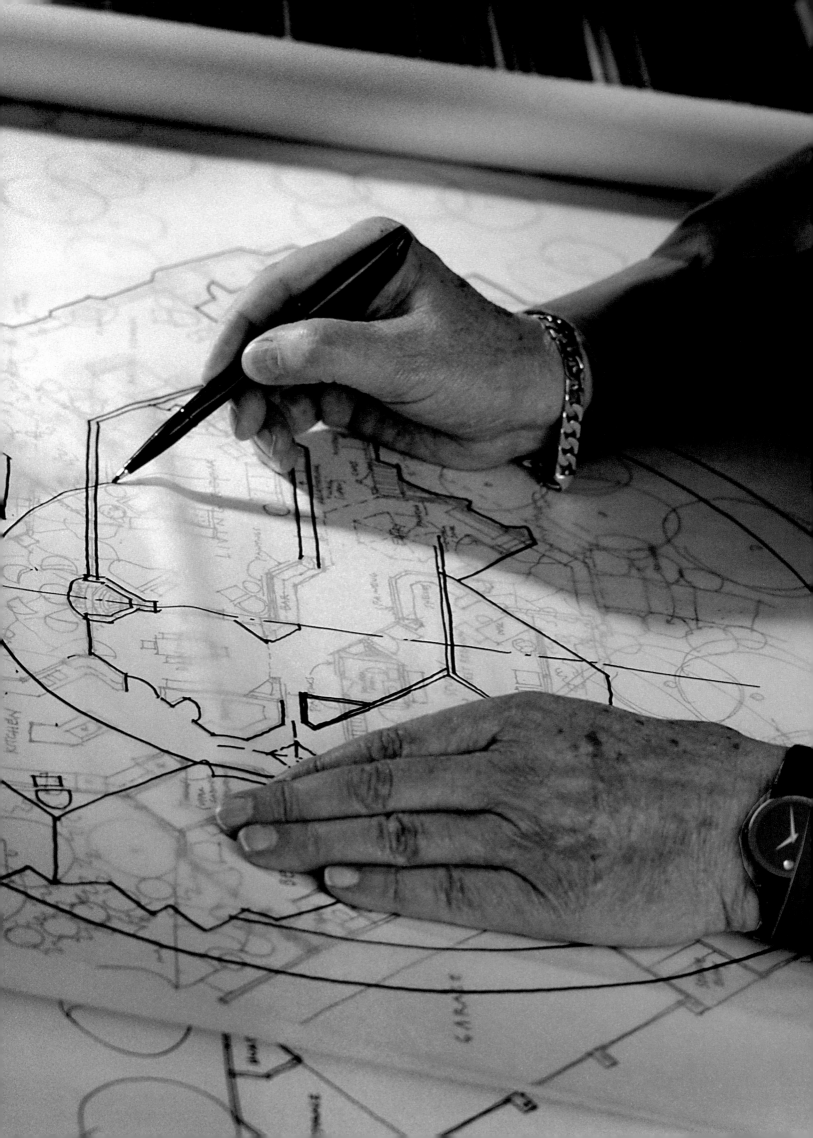

Dedicated to
all
who
design, build
or
dream
of having
a truly custom home

"I believe a house is more
a home by being a work of art."

– Frank Lloyd Wright

It's not houses
I love...
it's the life
I live in them.

-Gabrielle "Coco" Channel

Contents

The listings in red are a summary of the process

Foreword

To fully appreciate this book, it may be helpful to clarify what this book is not. Most architectural monographs are carefully annotated with the location, year of construction, and the owners' names of skillfully executed projects. In this work none of that is found because, most happily, the focus is elsewhere. It is not about the "designs" but rather, as the title implies, the activity or process of "designing." The text and photographs are intended to immerse the reader into something much more personal and intimate; including the spiritual, emotional, and physical experience of architecture. But beyond that, we might presume that it is the author's expectation that the reader will come to believe that the process of planning and building a home can be the most exciting, as well as personally rewarding, experience of one's life.

Vernon Swaback is extremely passionate about his craft, and that is very evident in both his words and his completed work. With the inclusion of numerous references to Frank Lloyd Wright, the preeminent American architect of the 20th century, the author continues a tradition of thoughtful and highly intelligent strategies for making homes, rather than houses. It should be no surprise to learn that the author apprenticed under that great master at an early age and worked closely with Mr. Wright for a number of years. The essence of Swaback's idealism, ideas, and work is clearly grounded from that mentorship and relationship.

There is an axiom among architects: "Great design and great buildings depend on great clients." The truth of this maxim is clear in the creation of great dwellings. As an educator, I can fully appreciate this truth. For architects to be successful and the creative process to yield extraordinary results, a knowledgeable and fully participatory client is critical. Toward achieving that understanding and end, this book is remarkably helpful.

Most of us have had memorable, if not moving, experiences that resulted from good design. Swaback attempts to draw on these highly positive emotions to invite the reader to dream of living such enriching experiences daily, and in fact, challenges us to do so. To experience through text and photographs a great home (and that is not the same thing as a large home) is to have but only a glimpse of the real thing. This is the inherent limitation of this medium that the author attempts to overcome on these pages— fortunately for us, he is indeed far more successful than others who have ventured along this path.

And there is another rather well worn axiom in our profession, "Form follows function." Well, not quite. As the reader will discover, form and function are very much intertwined, each directly affecting the other. The function of a home is extremely complex, probably more so than in any other building type. Yet the intangible aspects of function seldom equal the inherent ambiguity of form ("beauty is in the eye of the beholder …").

While lavishly illustrated, this book is not about showcasing the work of the author, nor is he expecting the reader to embrace these specific images and designs ("form"). Thus the photographs and drawings should not be assumed to be the message. Instead, the images are specifically intended to stimulate one's own exploration. While this book could not exist if it were not for the collected experiences of those who nurtured their ideas into the physical reality of a home, the intent is not so much about specific architects and clients as it is the mutually creative mystery of the process. The illustrations are expected to initiate the journey—not complete it. As we mentally explore and dream our way into a future that we shape for ourselves, the story following can be, hopefully, about us.

The beneficiaries of good design are, of course, each of us who has had the good fortune of a pleasing experience with the completed artifact. Those experiences are extremely varied, and are perceived through all of our senses. Vernon Swaback's approach to architecture seeks to touch the soul of desire, where everything is both personal and comprehensive. While the examples shown are probably beyond the reach of the average consumer, the intended message and principles are applicable to almost any economic circumstance. I would hope that all will come to better understand the profound reality that life itself can be enriched, if not ennobled, by the careful design of any dwelling or space. And that is certainly a goal worth seeking.

This book can be appreciated on several levels; the easiest of which is to simply enjoy its exceptional photography of resplendent homes. Going deeper the reader will find a passion and clarity that is only possible from an author who has lived his every word. At its deepest level this book is an invitation to explore our own dreams about life, made more rewarding by way of design.

Roger Schluntz, FAIA
Dean, School of Architecture and Planning
University of New Mexico

Partner to Nature: *On the following two pages, "Fallingwater," seen by day and by night, designed by Frank Lloyd Wright, 1935, Mill Run, Pennsylvania.*

Introduction

Those who know the thrill of creating an authentic custom home are among the world's elite. Two barriers have blocked entry into this realm: financial constraints and fear of the process. Little can be done about the fact that labor and materials cost whatever they cost, but harboring unfounded fears is another matter. The warnings against embarking on the pursuit of a one-of-a-kind house are legion, all spreading like wildfire from those who recount disappointments and traumas suffered at the hands of architects and builders.

This view became clear to me one evening at an elegant dinner in a home we had just completed. The conversation was progressing smoothly until the gentleman to my left realized that I was the architect for the house. Unable to contain his amazement, he blurted out to our host, "I thought you were suppose to hate your architect!" His comment reflects the misgivings of far too many people, who fearing all that might go wrong, settle for spending huge sums of money on a ready-made house, only to move into a generic design, denying themselves what could have been a wonderful adventure and a new and thrilling reality. The difference between what so many individuals have missed compared to the life-enriching experience that others have had, inspired this book.

After more than three decades of sharing the dreams of an uncommon diversity of people, it is overwhelmingly clear that to create a custom environment is one of life's most rewarding experiences. It is also the most demanding and personal of all architectural assignments. This book is an illustrated account of that intimately shared experience. It is a dialogue of dreams, including the methods, moods, and desires that set in motion a spiritual journey, shared by architect and client alike. It is about feelings at a level where anything is possible and the best is never obvious.

The word "house" is most often used to describe a structure, while the word "home" conveys a more emotional collection of relationships. This distinction might seem to make it more appropriate to think of designing a house than a home, but it is precisely this deeper sense of life that is the focus of this book. It goes beyond the arrangement of rooms, spaces, and things, to address the choices we make when shaping personal environments that influence how we live. It is about the pursuit of a personal ideal made real.

The truly custom home has two architects, one retained for that role, and the other, those who will inhabit the outcome. Design is a birth process in which the "parents" are more like participants in an unfolding mystery than producers of the results. I have on two occasions been stretched beyond the bounds of easy reality, crying in awe, while witnessing the miraculous birth of a child. Similar tears have flowed when experiencing the celebration of a new home, remembering that, not so long ago, there were only dreams and desire.

Beautiful houses have always inspired the imagination, including a growing interest in their deeper purpose. Books with titles like *Homes for Creative Living, The Temple in the House, Sensual Living, A Home for the Soul,* and *Home as a Mirror of Self,* convey an awareness that thoughtful design is ultimately inseparable from our physical and spiritual well-being.

Beyond theory, fashion, and systems, lies a deeper integration of space, sanctuary, and spirit. Beyond the basics of providing shelter and security, the custom home is an opportunity to create a highly personal world within the larger world we all share. The custom home is the single greatest opportunity for creating a bond between spiritual values, the beauty of nature, and the needs of everyday living.

Four influences have shaped my work and the philosophy expressed in this book. The first came from my parents who left an unquenchable belief that ideas should rest on something more grounded than mere opinion or taste. The second occurred during my teenage years in construction. To this day, my favorite smells are those of freshly cut wood, newly poured concrete, the wetness of plastered walls, and the aromas of oil-based finishes. The third influence was the extraordinary gift of being able to work at the side of Frank Lloyd Wright, where I took on his passion for the natural and the genuine. The fourth influence unfolded during more than 30 years of nurturing the dreams and desires of demanding clients. While no two have ever been alike, they have one quest in common—to create a place of excitement, purpose, and meaning.

This is a book for lovers—lovers of the natural environment, lovers of the creative process, and lovers of the sensuality that unites our spiritual being with the beauty of place. There are many "dream books" for children. Wonder and awe come easily before the cares of adulthood intrude to limit our notions as to what we believe to be possible. This is a dream book for adults. It is a celebration of those wordless feelings that serve as the first step toward a more beautiful reality.

The truly custom house is far more than an architectural concept, and certainly more than luxury or size. It is nothing less than an opportunity to take a positive hand in creation, all in pursuit of something that may cost a lot of money, but money alone could never buy.

Vernon D. Swaback, FAIA
Scottsdale, Arizona

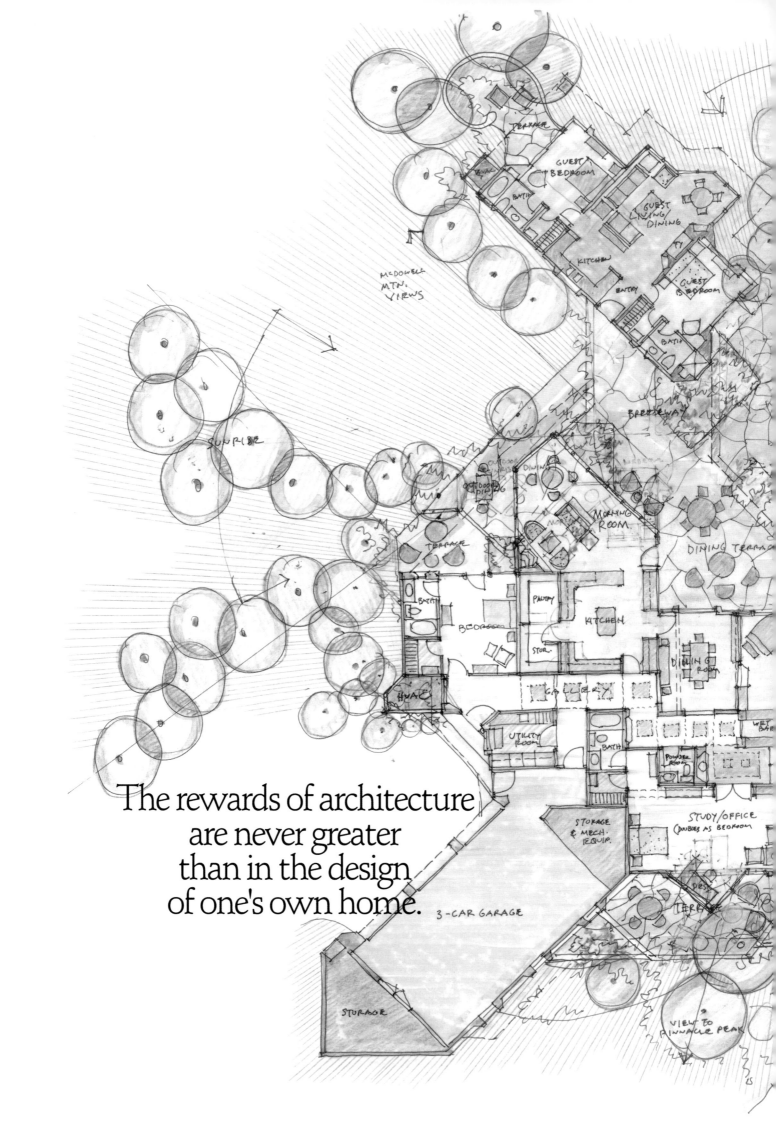

The rewards of architecture
are never greater
than in the design
of one's own home.

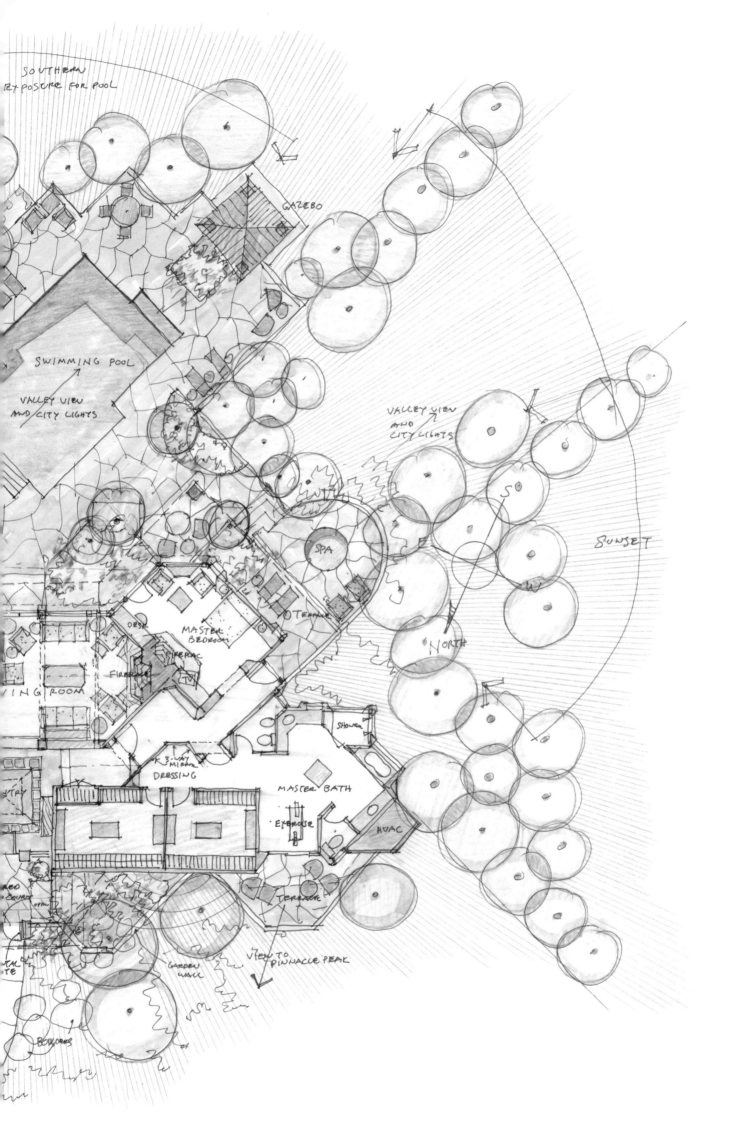

SOUTHERN
EXPOSURE FOR POOL

GAZEBO

SWIMMING POOL

VALLEY VIEW
AND CITY LIGHTS

VALLEY VIEW
AND
CITY LIGHTS

SUNSET

SPA

TERRACE

NORTH

DESK

MASTER
BEDROOM

FIREPLACE

FIREPLACE

LIVING ROOM

TV

SHOWER

3-WAY MIRROR

DRESSING

MASTER BATH

EXERCISE

HVAC

PANTRY

TERRACE

COVERED
COURT

VIEW TO
PINNACLE PEAK

GARDEN
WALL

BOULDERS

The Duality of Design

The philosophical side of design includes the inspiration which flows from spiritual and emotional sources having neither beginning nor end. This is the power of dreams from which all greatness is born. The other side is process—a sequential pattern of steps, usually beginning with two or three people (architect and client) followed by the continual addition of new participants, each one responsible for specific tasks within an overall framework. When done right, the process is every bit as exciting as the finished reality.

In writing this book, I have been well aware that not everyone will relate to all the text nor to every illustration. I know this because throughout the years, it has become common for our clients to think of their house as being the best, and in some cases they have gone so far as to say their house was the only good one we had ever designed. This is as it should be. We don't ask our clients to sign up for a product but for a journey, one so personal that it would be impossible to experience it without them, thus no two homes are ever alike.

This book is a free-flowing sharing of the kind of thoughts encountered while furthering the dreams of special people. For those who are more interested in process than philosophy, keep in mind the color of this page. There are twelve similarly colored pages, each addressing a step in the process, beginning with how to select an architect and ending with the experience of moving into the completed home. The organization of this book, for both process and philosophy, is summarized on the facing page.

Process

Selecting an Architect. This relationship has multiple facets. Think "marriage," and proceed with care.

Selecting a Builder. As soon as the approximate date for the start of construction can be determined, it is time to begin interviewing builders.

The Site. Everything starts with understanding the site's topography, vegetation, and views.

Establishing a Program. Unique to each opportunity are the individuals for whom the house is being designed.

The Plan. An exploration of possible relationships and their affect on the daily patterns of life.

Focusing on Character. Shaping the overall look and feel of the three-dimensional reality.

Specialists and Features. The use of selected consultants for a variety of purposes, all guided by a central idea.

Design Development. The phase where both the house and grounds are integrated into a coherent concept.

Construction Documents. The codification of all design elements with a clear and detailed set of drawings and specifications.

Permitting and Bidding. Securing competitive pricing from qualified contractors.

Construction. What has been words and drawings, now emerges as a new reality.

Moving In. As everything is brought to completion, a construction site evolves into a very personal environment.

Philosophy

Ideas are a powerful resource but unlike the clear sequence of "Process," they do not lend themselves to step-by-step or how-to-do-it procedures. What can be shared is a sense of the underlying feelings for each aspect of the work along with examples to illustrate the intent.

Chapters One and Two discuss the desire for personal expression, and why imitation should be avoided, no matter how much we may admire the past.

Chapters Three and Four explore the process and mystery of the design experience.

Chapters Five and Six look at the art of luxury as something essential to health and well-being. Sensuality is a quality that can be felt in spaces that add joy to life.

Chapter Seven includes the live, work, and play environments that the author has designed for his own family, friends, and colleagues. There is no greater education for an architect than to experience the consequences of his or her own designs.

Chapter Eight portrays the idea of integral ornamentation, including custom hardware, branch holders, murals, millwork, fire, fountains, and gardens.

Chapter Nine extends the idea of "home" into the design of family compounds and legacy estates.

To copy the past
is to abandon
the journey,
before it begins

1

"Would that we admired the past more,
and imitated it less."
– The Book of Tea

The Thrill of Creation

It is easy to be inspired by Mayan ruins, Gothic cathedrals, French châteaux, and Italian villas. Equally inspiring to the artifacts themselves is to remember that there was a time when these cherished creations existed solely as the dreams of individuals whose imaginations and commitments created a new reality. For our time, we are those individuals.

Historic styles in their most genuine settings can be breathtakingly beautiful. It is not surprising that we may think about re-creating what is so charming, but imitation is always a lost opportunity. At their most dynamic, all periods of history have been a reaching toward the future, and so it must be for anyone who aspires to create something of lasting value.

Individuality, character, and courage are all required to trust oneself enough to go beyond the comfort of familiarity. At its best, the custom home is a large-scale expression of one's feelings about life, conveying what its creators believe about who they are.

Few opportunities compare with designing the custom home for the excitement of personal fulfillment. Unlike the purchase of ready-made planes, boats, or cars, the custom home is an individual creation in which the look and feel of centuries can be combined in ever-new and magical ways. The choices we make are drawn from a sea of possibilities. To design well is to distill those possibilities into the one most perfect reality.

The imagination

imitates.

It is the critical spirit

that creates.

– Oscar Wilde

Inspiration from the Past

The world's collection of historic and beautiful structures serve as living inspiration to stir our imaginations, that we might leave our mark, just as others have left theirs.

The images on this page are from Portugal, Mexico, and Spain. What they suggest is that shocking or merely curious designs are not the ones that endure. The test of time is on the side of the beautiful, and more often than not, the most beautiful designs are those that achieve subtle, near-magical relationships to their individual settings.

At the top of the facing page is the main house and gardens of Villa Ephrussi de Rothchild in Cap Ferrat, France. The lower photo is the Patio de la Acequia at the Generalife, just outside the Alhambra in Granada, Spain. One is delicate and brightly colored, the other a more subdued country home. Both are celebrations of grace and beauty. It is not one style that endures above the rest as much as it is any design that radiates imagination and balance, all with a clarity of proportion and purpose. The best designs are their own most compelling testimony. They represent an authenticity that speaks directly to our soul.

Selecting an Architect

The first step is to be clear about what level of service best suits your needs. This is critical because the range of construction costs along with related fees for architectural and engineering services vary as widely as the costs for cars, airplanes, or boats. Thus, you will need to match your own abilities and expectations with those of the architect.

Several architects should be interviewed to broaden your understanding of the differences between one firm and another. You are about to engage in a long-term relationship. Like marriage, client and architect are either right for each other, or it is not going to work. The exploratory interviews should focus on philosophy with just enough discussion about process to begin an understanding of the steps involved.

Ask for references whose programs are most similar to your own. Among other questions, you might want to ask the following:

1   How responsive was the architect at each stage of the work?

2   Did you ever receive bills you did not expect, or was everything clearly spelled out in advance?

3   Do you feel that you ended up with "your" house or a version of something out of the architect's past?

4   How would you rate the firm's performance in terms of creativity, technical details, follow-through, as well as their ability to provide leadership throughout the overall process?

The most important question of all is not about what the architect has done for others, but what he or she will now do for you. What the firm has done for others, in other places, at other times, and possibly with other staff, has merit, but the real questions are, what will they now do for you, and who are the individuals that will be at your side from start to finish?

You are in search of a translator for your dreams who will fashion your future and you are looking for someone who will share the benefit of their lifetime experience while never forgetting that, this time, the focus is on you.

While you are trying to learn whether or not the architect can provide what you need, the architect will have the same questions about you. Designing a house is one of the most personally time-intensive involvements any firm can accept. The best architects will not commit themselves to anyone who is not thoroughly enthusiastic about the relationship and fully capable of doing their part.

In addition to creativity, be certain that you select a firm capable of providing meticulous service. Last but not least, you are selecting a leader. By training, experience, and involvement, the architect is the team member most qualified to coordinate the activities of all other participants. With respect to personal chemistry, keep in mind that you are also selecting a partner, one who must not only excel at what they do best, but who has the ability to listen at a deeper level to what you say. In this regard, it would be a good idea to select an architect who may, at times, be called upon to protect you from yourself.

Timeless Beauty: *Is the design on the facing page traditional or modern? The finest architecture makes no such distinction. This use of stone is as natural as that found in nature, thus nature and architecture become one. The entry to Frank Lloyd Wright's Taliesin is as orchestrated as a theatrical performance.*

Selecting a Builder

Many people think the only way to select a builder is to put a good set of drawings and specifications out for competitive bids followed by picking the low bidder. The problem with this approach is that some of the best builders will not participate and the odds of the apparent low bid being in your best interests can be similar to playing Russian roulette. The alternative is to pre-select a builder by interviewing three or more firms, all of which have a track record of completing custom homes generally analogous to the quality and complexity of what you intend to build.

The first thing most builders will tell you is that they don't do things the way everyone else does, instead they do them differently and better. In 30 years, I have never heard a builder say, "We're just like everybody else, only not as good." Thus, rather than assertions of quality, what you need to hear from a builder is all more specific.

1   What is the background of the firm? How many years in business? What is the extent of their staff? Ask for financial information on the organization.

2   How will the job be run? Will there be a full time superintendent, and who is that person? You will want to interview all the key participants.

3   Call the builder's references, including those representing both his early and more recent engagements.

4   When you find someone you feel you could select, the questions get more specific. Ask for an itemized "Conceptual Budget Estimate," based on what the builder's experience suggests a house like yours might cost.

5   Ask the builder to stipulate how they will handle profit and overhead and general conditions. What you want is a conceptual budget outline that includes every dollar that you will pay, including testing, permits, and sales tax.

6   Ask to review their proposed documents, including the Owner/Builder Contract, and all other forms or documents proposed for each aspect of the work.

7   Request a beginning-to-end schedule, with the approximate percentage of the total cost to be paid out during each month of construction. While the builder can't know how this will play out for your house, you are asking for information based on his past experience, and it is because he has that knowledge, that you are interested in working with him.

No matter how clear your requests have been, when you receive the builders' responses, they will have presented their proposals in formats that require analysis. Your architect should now be asked to lay everything out on a matrix or spreadsheet, until the proposals are clearly comparable. In addition to procedures relating to scheduling and costs, you will want to establish the conditions and time frames for whatever warranties and guarantees are being provided. You will now have information and impressions that can be evaluated analytically, as well as on a more person-to-person basis.

While the builder will be following a prescribed set of drawings and specifications, you are still entering into a relationship that will rely on more than a contract. Like your architect, the builder you select should be someone for whom you feel both confidence and respect.

Understanding the Site

No two sites are the same and each one provides a major source of information, including everything from its natural characteristics to its potential in terms of human constraints and opportunities.

1   Understanding the site starts with obtaining a boundary and topographic survey. The survey should show one- foot contours and identify all major vegetation and rock outcroppings, as well as constructed features, including walls, fences, roads, and structures, whether or not they are to remain. A soil survey will be required and for some sites, a drainage study.

2   The architect will prepare a site analysis to consider views to be captured, as well as views to be screened or altogether blocked.

3   The analysis will chart the path of the sun, prevailing air currents, and weather characteristics.

4   Vegetation in proximity to building areas should be identified by species, height, caliper, and condition.

5   Any homeowner's association restrictions, and all easements, ordinance and code requirements need to be located and evaluated.

6   The nature of the site will suggest whether or not to consider the use of two or more levels during the conceptual design.

7   The site analysis will be used to influence major decisions, including orientation, alignment of the entry drive, guest parking and garage, as well as the approach to the front door and outdoor living areas.

To begin the process by analyzing the site is to give all work to follow a conceptual foundation based on something deeper than personal preference. A sample listing of 12 site observations is shown on page 39.

The inspiration
for all things custom
is a shared dream
between architect
and client

*"It is the relationship of all things
that creates value."*
– Frank Lloyd Wright

The Home as High Art

We travel all over the world to stand in awe of a few square feet of painted canvas, trying to match our emotions and insights with those of artists we will never meet. We seem willing to believe that something significant should be sensed within the framed bounds of these individual works of art. Most of all, we value that which is original.

It is regrettably rare that such accord is given to the spaces in which we spend our sojourn on earth. The notion of utility—a place to sleep, a place to brush our teeth, a place to cook, a place to store our cars—all seem more pragmatic, thus less deserving of awe and wonder. Perhaps our houses are more practical than poetic, more utilitarian than utopian, more mechanical than mysterious, but to the extent this is true, it is sad testimony to how artless daily life can be.

Learning from Nature

Wherever we look in nature we find details related to the greater whole and surprises are the norm. We marvel at nature's realities, both smaller and larger than we easily comprehend, and what we do not understand with our thoughts, we sense with our soul. Everything has a purpose and that which is most functional is also most beautiful, the extraordinary variety and exquisite design of seashells being just one example.

Humans have a tendency to value the pieces more than the whole. We value the specialist above the generalist and the narrower the specialty, the more esteemed. The subdivided lot, walled off from the ecosystem that gives it life, brings a higher price than the once open terrain. The soloist is valued above the orchestra. The piecemeal manipulation of a life long gone is valued more than the actual life of the person when in his or her fullness. Stained glass windows from a Frank Lloyd Wright house can be sold for a greater price than the entire house which permits no such manipulation. Pieces of corporations can be liquidated at a higher value than that accorded the totality that created the pieces. On a global scale, what we observe as environmental threats are often the result of valuing short range, fragmented interests above the long range whole.

For most of us, these issues are not our battles, nor can any one of us easily alter the prevailing patterns at play, except in what we build for ourselves. That is what makes the design of our homes such a magnificent exploration. It is where we can achieve a subtle balance between our personal desires and that which is appropriate to the environment. It is where we can create a radiant symphony of richly proportioned spaces that are models of artfulness, bringing joy beyond what few other experiences can bring.

Our homes can become significant, three-dimensional works of art. For those who are able to create such a home, to miss the experience should be unthinkable. The scale of the individual house is our most controllable wholeness. It is the unit of life most within our grasp. To design a custom home is to explore living with authenticity, with dignity, and in as much beauty as our means and insights permit.

Wordless Sensations

The soul of beauty requires no defense. If our appreciation of a design depends on describing its pedigree, its underlying theory or how difficult it was to build, something is missing. The bloom of fresh fruit, the color and geometry of fragrant flowers, the warmth and aroma of scented candles, the dynamic lapping of flames, the sparkle and sounds of moving water, or the play of light and shade, all provide delight beyond words. They are the sensations that add richness and wholeness to life. In like manner, genuine expressions of structure, shelter, and purpose are all deeply felt without explanation.

Created objects are most beautiful when we sense the love and mastery of their creators. Colors are beautiful not only for their isolated hues, but because of their influence on each other. Small spaces, passageways, and grand rooms all are made more beautiful by how they interact to orchestrate what we feel. In the search for beauty it is the totality that gives value to its parts, far beyond what they could ever be in themselves.

Anything that screams out for attention will likely get it, but the more obvious the impact, the shorter our interest. Popular songs may briefly eclipse the classics before disappearing forever. The excitement of architecture is not that of the popular song, nor is it to imitate the classics. It is a search for authenticity that creates the classics of the future.

The tonality and placement of every stroke in a great painting, like the relationships between each note in a symphony, are critical to the enduring success of the work. How much more so for every form, plane, color, detail, texture, and space that make up our daily environments.

The architecture of "home" is something different than constructing roofs and walls. It is far more than style, although it must have style in abundance. It is more than structure and shelter, although it must celebrate both. Most of all, it must transcend the notion of being someone's "concept." The design of your home should be the most important work of art you will ever encounter. It is nothing less than your energy, your spirit, and your future expressed in physical form. The timeless principles that underlie all pursuits of lasting value are a gift, not only for the initial creators, but for generations to come.

"You use a glass mirror

to see your face:

you use works of art

to see your soul."

– George Bernhard Shaw

Intimate Spaces: *Thoughtful design comes in all sizes. Arranged as a cozy space, this integrated design includes a kitchenette, work and conference areas, and a mezzanine library accessible by a circular stair beyond the audiovisual wall to the left.*

Siting and Human Scale: *The above house was designed to nestle comfortably into a hillside so steep that many thought the site to be impossible to build upon. The house on the facing and following four pages is expansive but by way of varying ceiling heights and other architectural devices, even the largest forms and spaces have a human scale.*

Creative exploration
is a treasure hunt
for which the prize
is a new reality

3

"If we begin with certainties, we shall end in doubts; but if we begin with questions, and are patient in them, we shall end in certainties."

– Francis Bacon

The Journey Begins

Architecture is all about cause and effect. The ability to know what works and what does not is a matter for lifelong study. Less rational but equally important, is the wisdom of uncertainty.

My architectural studio is a place of confidence based on decades of experience. My partners, associates, and staff have seen it all, at least until the next client walks through the door, then everything is once again new, including a new site and new dreams. Without the will to push beyond the comfort of one's past, these new opportunities would be reduced to repeating some version of what had already been designed for others.

The starting point for our exploration is rooted in studying each site. The diagram to the right and the corresponding listing below indicate the range of information that can be observed:

1   Best mountain views.
2   Slope of the natural topography.
3   Potential driveway approach.
4   Neighboring views to be blocked.
5   General location for the house.
6   Path of the winter sun.
7   Path of the summer sun.
8   High window mountain views.
9   Primary ocean and beach views.
10 Prevailing wind direction.
11 Primary views of the house itself.
12 Rock forms and compass direction.

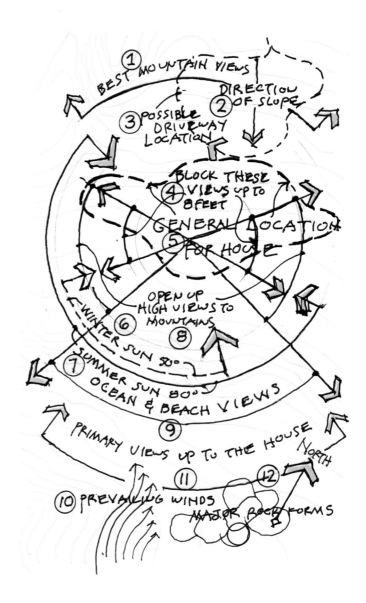

Establishing a Program

There are many ways in which clients may choose to inform the architect of their desires. Here are four actual examples:

1　A couple from Bremerton, Washington sent a series of voice recordings, effectively talking their house into existence with messages like, "We're sitting in the living room, where we can see the golf course, have an intimate conversation, or look directly into an open kitchen where our guests like to congregate."

2　A client from Thailand communicated by email, using mainly one-liners, each starting with "We wish." For example, "We wish for a private garden off our master suite," and "We wish for interiors flooded with natural light coming in from at least two directions." When they were particularly pleased with something in the last round of drawings, they would respond with increasingly larger type.

3　Other clients bring magazine clippings and detailed lists including the sizes of all rooms in their present house, together with comments concerning what they want to be different in their new home.

4　Then there was a woman from New York who communicated her directions in just seven words, "Do a house that makes me smile." Her husband did most of the talking while she provided most of the inspiration.

The end result of establishing a program is to have a comprehensive list of all space needs, each related to their desired functions and adjacencies. It is a listing which addresses all desired elements in terms of how much, how many, and where?

Whatever form the initial client instructions may take, they serve as an opening volley to be followed with continuing dialogue, exploration, and definition until all elements of the design can be fully identified.

Recording Impressions

After the site has been studied, but before thinking about what the design of their home might be, we ask our clients to describe what they hope to accomplish. If they have a beautiful site and a reasonable budget, it is likely that they will end up with a worthy result. What is not so likely is that they will end up with the most perfect solution to the exclusion of every other possibility that might have been. This exploratory commitment is what distinguishes the truly custom home from one that is merely expensive.

We begin by asking questions that become an outline of everything desired. At first it all sounds so pragmatic. "How many bedrooms? Describe your dream master bath. Do you need sound separation so that two social events can take place at once or, other than for bedrooms and baths, can the house be one open space? Where do you want to have fireplaces, computers, and televisions? Must your bedroom be easily darkened or do you want to wake up with the sun? Describe your ideal kitchen. Do you prefer casement-type or sliding patio doors—wood or metal? How many garage spaces and what are your storage needs?" This line of questioning is where husband and wife, not only voice their shared desires, but begin to discover their differences.

There is no way to avoid conflicting ideas. In the case of one couple, we quickly realized that the man was dreaming of a sprawling hacienda while his wife was describing a more compact, almost townhouse-like dwelling, all-the-while seeming to each other as though they were in full agreement. After a period of helping them work through their differences, the man said, "Had we known your services included psychological counseling, we would have come to you a lot sooner!"

Beyond questions concerning the number, type, and adjacencies of all spaces, there are exploratory questions designed to produce a different kind of information. For example, if we feel the client is being too restricted in their answers, we may ask, "If you weren't thinking about resale, what special spaces and relationships would mean most to you? What have you had in the past that you no longer need or want? What have you always wished for but never had?"

Questions relating more to behavior, include asking the clients to think of airplanes, boats, and resort accommodations where they have experienced uncommon convenience, efficiency, or luxury. We may ask that they forget formal or standard room designations, in order to imagine spaces that provide for one or more uses of importance to them. We ask that they reconsider their past possessions and habits. What changes might allow for a better way to address their future needs?

We assist our clients in visualizing ideal room sizes, ceiling heights, and proportional relationships. It takes little insight to make everything large. It is more difficult but far better to search for optimal sizes, being neither too large nor too small.

Performance-type questions include, "Have you had rooms or spaces in prior homes that were unused?" Do you know what your monthly energy bills were? What are your feelings about the use of daylighting, cross ventilation, shading devices, and energy-saving systems? What level of control systems are you familiar with for security, lighting, audiovisual, and mechanical equipment?" We then discuss a variety of systems before arriving at solutions that best suit their desires.

Designing Your Life

The plan is the purest place to design what most perfectly suits your intended way of life. It is where ideas, needs, and desires can be explored without being sidetracked by premature considerations for style or appearance. It is the place to raise and answer key questions that become the basis for everything to follow.

1   What spaces and sizes are to be provided for inside the house as well as for all exterior areas?

2   What would be the most favorable adjacencies?

3   Is the plan to be formal or informal, symmetrical or more reflexive?

4   Are multi-use spaces desired; for example, can the living, dining, and kitchen areas share an open space or are they to be separate rooms? If open spaces are desired, how open, and if separate, how separate?

5   Where are recurring provisions to be located, including televisions, fireplaces, and computers?

6   Will there be any need for separate entertainment areas where the sounds from one area can be isolated from the others?

7   Is the house to be a single structure or might there be separate buildings; for example, guest houses, a pool pavilion, tennis cabana, children's playhouse, shop, or office?

Your architect should be sufficiently experienced in matters of interior design to have even the earliest plans shown fully furnished. This is not to prejudge the ultimate furniture layouts, but rather to portray the overall circulation, scale, and "feel" of each space. Everything about the plan drawings should be designed to assist you in understanding what you are seeing. For example, if you are having trouble visualizing a space, ask your architect to take you to already built rooms and spaces where you can experience the intended dimensions.

The process starts with simple "bubble diagrams" like that on the facing page. Page 45 shows more detailed plans, and the degree of study that goes into finding "that one most perfect plan" is shown on pages 46 and 47.

Everything Starts in Plan

The beginning process of design is a time of bringing forth feelings that will eventually evolve into thoughts which then become words and ideas. With as accurate a translation as possible, what begins as a sense of something desired becomes a place that shapes and nurtures the original feeling. Home and the life within become a living system.

As they settle into their newly created environments, I have had the repeated joy of watching people say, "I love this house," and saying it with a passion that would normally be reserved for expressing feelings about another human being.

The most essential step in arriving at such a perfect fit is to start with the plan and stay at the plan level for as long as it takes to dream, test, and refine everything desired into a coherent idea. Arriving at the right plan happens in plateaus. The more time spent in a kind of trial-and-error exploration, the more insights emerge that may not have been initially clear. The work starts with broad generalities recorded in simple diagrams. This is followed by a series of plans used as a background to facilitate more detailed discussion.

Of all the consultants, the interior designer should be added to the team as soon as the first layouts begin to emerge. This is especially true if the designer and the client have worked together before. For the client, the interior designer represents another set of eyes to test and refine their own impressions. For the architect, the designer may raise questions that go beyond the unexamined enthusiasm that can occur when viewing preliminary concepts.

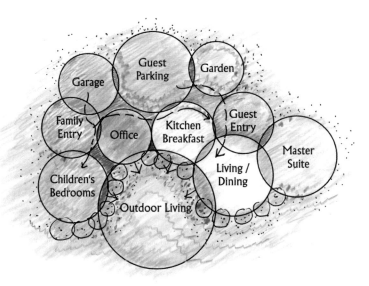

Relationship diagrams are used to explore patterns for more detailed planning to follow. Such diagrams provide a graphic summary of client desires. For example, the above diagram indicates that guests will walk through a garden before arriving at the entry. The children's rooms, office, kitchen, breakfast, living, dining, and master suite will all have views and access to outdoor living areas. The master and children's bedrooms will occur on opposite ends of the house and the family entry will be directly accessible to the kitchen, office, and children's room.

Even at this early stage, the diagram indicates a desire for a strong connection between all interior and exterior spaces. The circles are not meant to imply anything about the eventual shapes of the house or rooms. Relationship diagrams are strictly about first exploring then establishing what goes where.

Beyond the Obvious

The initial questions are designed to give beginning clarity without making judgments that may rule out possibilities yet to be discovered. We avoid asking how any objectives are to be achieved. To create exciting spaces and relationships, while also accommodating the more detailed needs of the client on their selected site, is strictly the job of the architect.

The process is much like throwing a ball back and forth. Each time we meet, the clients' see more work performed on their behalf. Their further responses allow us to learn more about what makes them unique. Our task is to stay open, to listen for clues, however subtle, and to go over each point as often as necessary to be certain that the ultimate result is everything it should be. The interview sequence starts with words that may only hint at where the process will lead, including a discussion of alternative plans and ultimately some sense of three-dimensional form, structure and space.

Questions are used to determine preferred materials, plan shapes, and spatial relationships. We address whether or not to have differing floor levels. We explore provisions for the storage of clothing, books, food, and specialty items which vary with each client. We discuss requirements for home offices, entertainment, hobbies, artwork, music, and pets. There is no standard list of questions, because there are no standard clients, but the questions tend to fall into two broad categories: the pragmatic and the philosophic. On the pragmatic side, is the need to plan for the desired quantities of hanging rods, shoe shelves, tie racks, pantry and bookshelves, wine racks, information and entertainment technology as well as provisions for general storage.

Where it gets to be fun is exploring beyond the pragmatic. The precise words are always different, but in whatever way is most appropriate to the character of the client, we may ask that they imagine hearing their new home calling to them, saying:

> *"If you want to prepare food, dine, or entertain—here is where you can do so with greater efficiency and pleasure than you have ever before experienced. If you want to work, play, or take time to exercise your body—you will be at home doing these things here. And most of all, if you want to experience the timeless energy and peace of the natural environment, your home will be your inspiration and friend. It will enhance the way you see each day and season. It will dance and play with your senses. It is all part of your journey... may it be a celebration."*

By the time the interviews are over, we know more about our clients' needs and desires than they have ever had reason to share or understand about themselves. This is the jumping-off place for everything to follow. With their program established, and while studying possibilities with respect to views, topography, and the character of the site, all parties begin to see everything at a deeper level. A ferment has begun–architect and client are now fully engaged in the co-creative process of design.

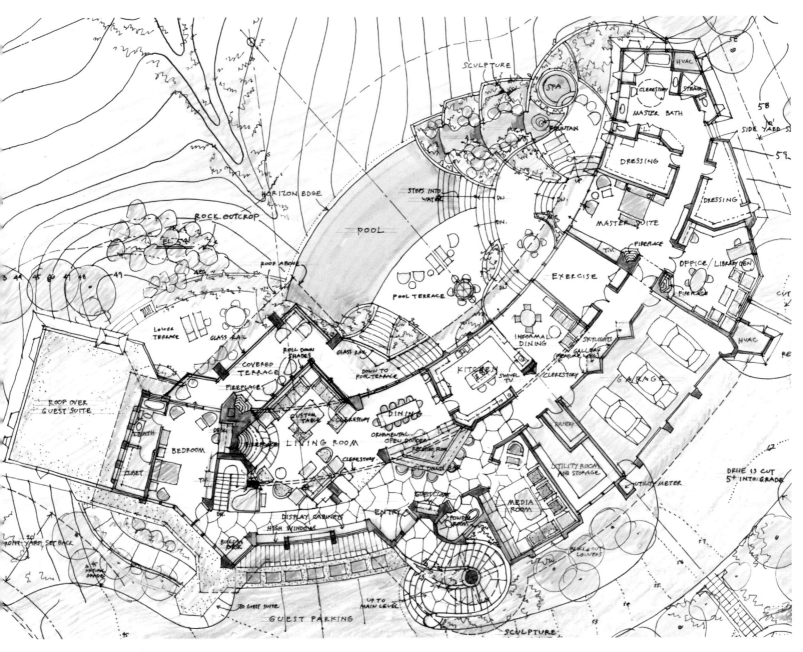

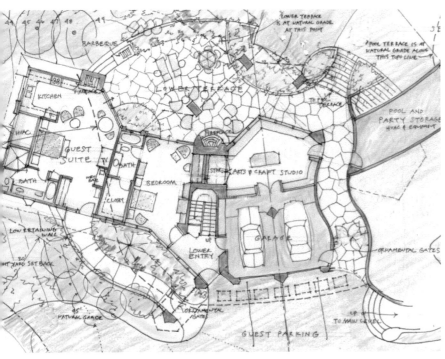

Living in the Plan: *These upper and lower level plans were designed for a sloping site with a garage entry occurring at both levels. The overall plan was curved in response to the topography and to optimize panoramic views out to a golf course and mountain range beyond.*

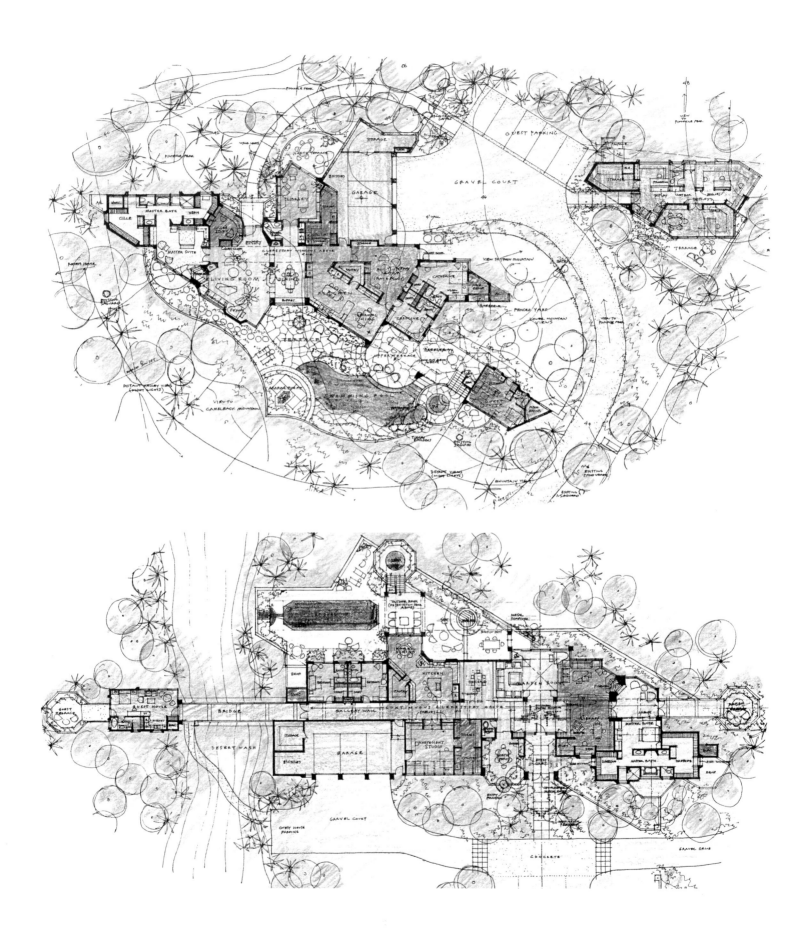

"Never leave well enough alone." – Raymond Loewy

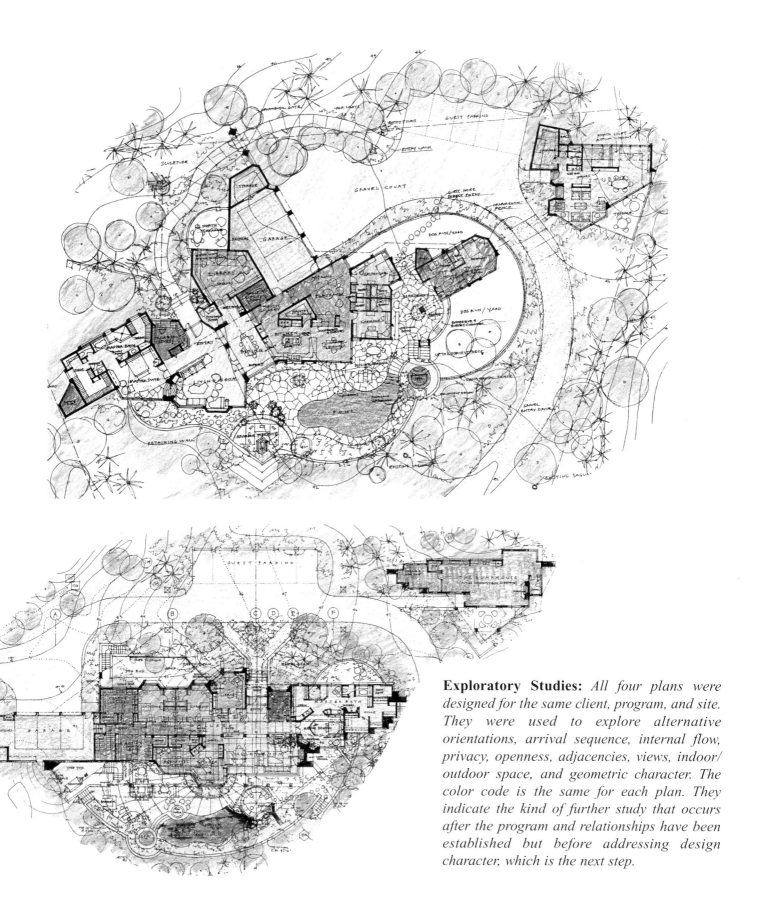

Exploratory Studies: *All four plans were designed for the same client, program, and site. They were used to explore alternative orientations, arrival sequence, internal flow, privacy, openness, adjacencies, views, indoor/ outdoor space, and geometric character. The color code is the same for each plan. They indicate the kind of further study that occurs after the program and relationships have been established but before addressing design character, which is the next step.*

Focusing on Character

To convey their desires about character and design, some people refer to historic styles. Others prefer more abstract terms like, "warm and inviting," "gallery-like," "minimalist," or "organic." No matter how one chooses to state their preferred direction, the most authentic designs will grow out of four considerations:

1 The character of the region; for example, coastal, alpine, forest, great plains, prairie, or desert.

2 In addition to an appropriate regional direction, there will be a convincing relationship to the nature of the specific site.

3 The design character will be an authentic expression of the plan, the intended structural system, and all selected materials.

4 Last but not least, the character should express and nurture the feelings of those for whom the house is being designed.

Because each site and client inspire their own direction, the above principles can produce dramatically varied results. Compare, for example, the carpenter-crafted hillside home on page 32, with the more classical and symmetrical house on pages 33 to 37. Other comparisons include the use of tall brick piers on page 67 with the horizontal and multi-layered forms on pages 68 and 69, or the more high-finish, sophisticated character on pages 137 to 139. The more a design belongs to its setting and the more convincing it is in being its own special place, the less likely it will fall prey to the look of passing infatuations that become so easily dated.

Character, Materials and Form: *Each material has its own quality to be respected in the design. Stone should always appear to be massive, while wood, fabric, and even concrete may appear to float. Examples on the facing page illustrate the varied use of stone, glass, stucco, wood, fabric, copper, concrete, fluted masonry, rammed earth, and brick.*

Specialists and Features

Certain provisions are standard for most architectural firms, including plumbing, mechanical, electrical, and structural engineering. Even when architects offer one or more of the following services, it may still be advisable to consider other consultants before making a final selection.

1 Landscaping and irrigation.
2 Interior design.
3 Lighting for house and grounds.
4 Security system.
5 Audiovisual systems.
6 Telecommunication.
7 Home theater.
8 Energy management.
9 Integrated controls.
10 Kitchen planner.
11 Closet designer.
12 Selected artisans for pools, fountains, sculpture, glass art, and furnishings.

Everyone involved must be a team player, all intensely focused on the client's needs and desires, not on their own territorial egos. No amount of talent can make up for what is lost if a key participant fails to be part of a highly coordinated effort.

The architect's role, with respect to all special consultants, occurs at three levels. The first is to help the client select the most qualified participants and to bring them into the team at the earliest, appropriate time.

The second is to be sufficiently versed in each specialty in order to help the client avoid buying into anything that sounds good, but isn't likely to be as useful as it sounds and may even become a detriment. An example would be to arrive at the most beneficial level of complexity for all control systems rather than doing everything technically possible.

The third role is to oversee all elements of design. The goal is not to end up with the world's most extraordinary fountain or chandelier, but rather to create a great symphony, in which each element adds to the richness and excitement of the whole.

Drawings and Models

No architect, worthy of the name, ever loses the thrill of imagining dreams into reality. The same is true of the best clients. Children know the feeling of losing themselves in the fascination of making drawings and models. This sense of wonder is felt by client and architect alike, the difference being that we get to one day walk through full-scale versions of our dreams. It would be difficult to think of anything more enjoyable than the opportunity to bring feelings to life, in support of life itself.

The Third Dimension: *Both the site plan to the right and the perspective drawing below are accurate, but the model at the bottom is used to study more clearly how the house is terraced in and around massive boulders on its foothill's site.*

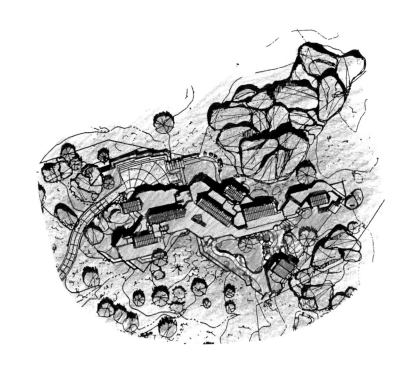

RETAINING
GREEN WALL

GUEST PARKING

47

48

49

50

ENTRY COURT

51.5

GUEST HOUSE
WALK

GARAGE

STOR.

ORNAMENTAL GATE

STORAGE

STORAGE

HVAC

UTILITY
ROOM

BATH

BEDROOM
TV

PANTRY

STOR.

51.5

SWIVEL

ORNAMENTAL
GATE

OFFICE

PLAYING ROOM

BATH

CLO.

BEDROOM

COVERED TERRACE

GUEST
SUITE

SEAT

55.6

BATH

CLO.

FIREPLACE

FOUNTAIN &
CASCADE

HVAC

BEDROOM

TERRACE

BARBEQUE

P

TERRACE

BUILT-IN SEAT

40

48

39

47

38

46

37

45

36

44

43

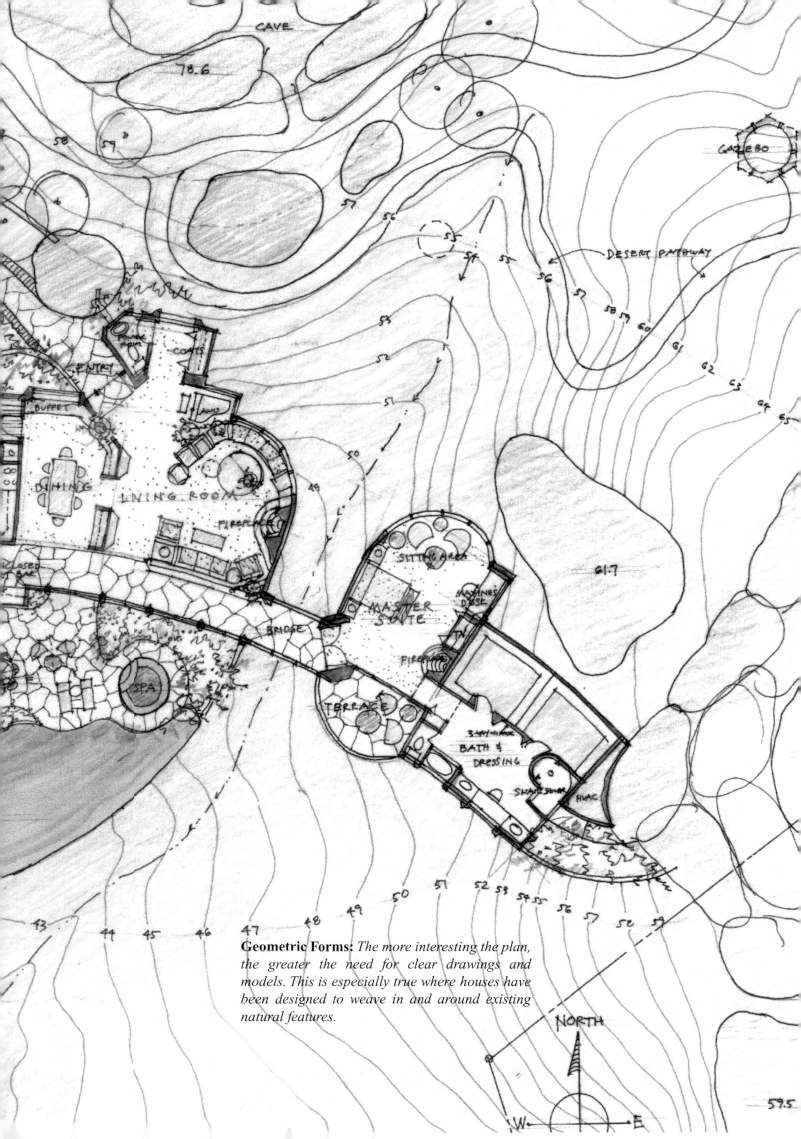

CAVE

78.6

GAZEBO

DESERT PATHWAY

ENTRY

POWDER
ROOM

COATS

BUFFET

ISLAND

DINING

LIVING ROOM

FIREPLACE

SITTING AREA

MADELINES DESK

MASTER
SUITE

CLOSED
TRACK

FIREPLACE

BRIDGE

TERRACE

SPA

BATH &
DRESSING

SHOWER

HVAC

61.7

59.5

NORTH

W   E

Geometric Forms: *The more interesting the plan, the greater the need for clear drawings and models. This is especially true where houses have been designed to weave in and around existing natural features.*

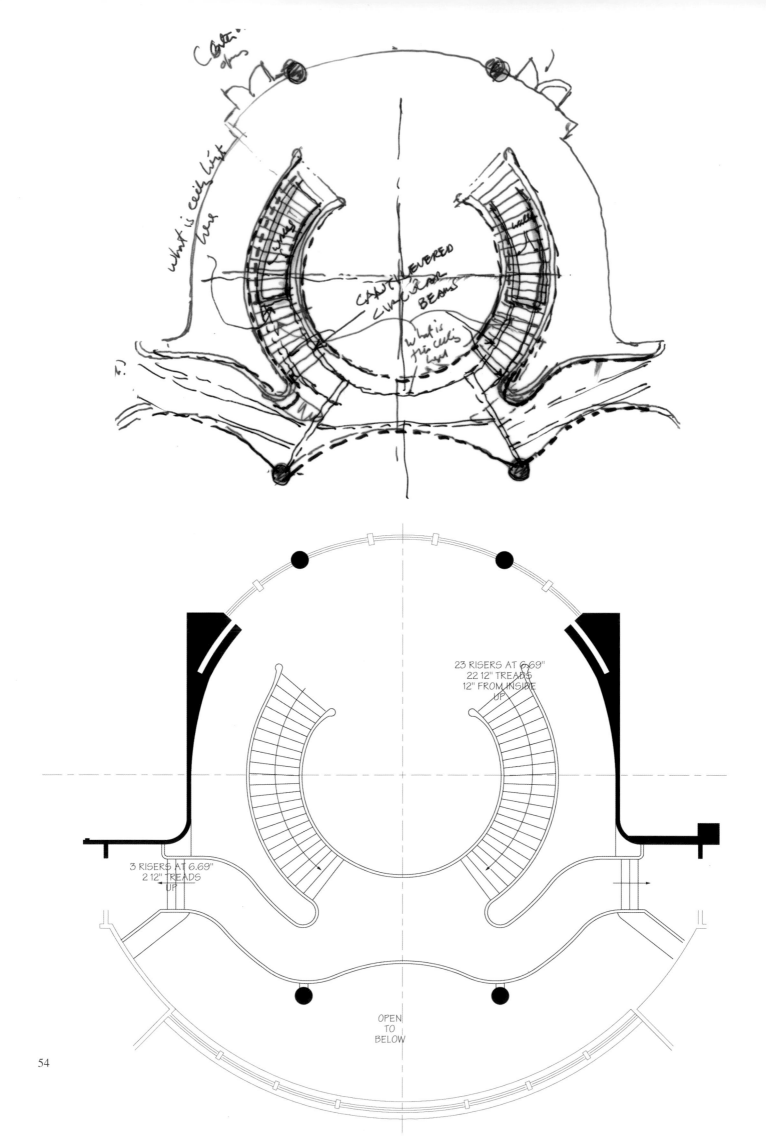

23 RISERS AT 6.69"
22 12" TREADS
12" FROM INSIDE
UP

3 RISERS AT 6.69"
2 12" TREADS
UP

OPEN
TO
BELOW

Levels of Study: *The sketch plan at the top of the facing page is the original design for an entry rotunda. Below it is the computer-generated version of the same design and a model of the three-dimensional space is shown above. Drawings and models like these are all tools for studying and refining the desired spatial intent.*

Three Scales of Visualization: *The line drawing to the right shows the use of columns and arches as they will appear in the overall context of the house. The photograph on the far right is a full-size mock-up, built to experience the actual scale of the repeating arches. Colored renderings, like the above, are prepared to illustrate the intended feeling at completion.*

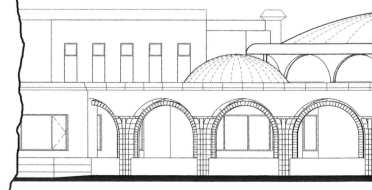

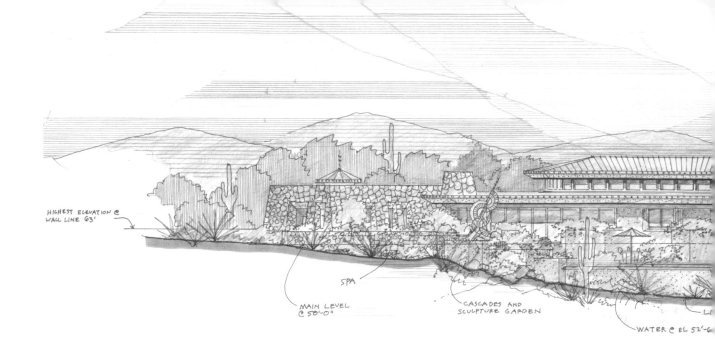

HIGHEST ELEVATION @
WALL LINE 63'

SPA

MAIN LEVEL
@ 50'-0"

CASCADES AND
SCULPTURE GARDEN

WATER @ EL 52'-6

From Drawings to Reality: *The drawing at the top of the page was made before any engineering or detailed development of the design took place. If you look carefully, there are differences between the conceptual design and the completed house shown to the right, but not many. This is the mark of a thoroughly considered concept. A good design is one based on a series of intuitive judgments that later engineering and detailing will confirm rather than change. The same house can be seen from the other side on pages 72 and 73.*

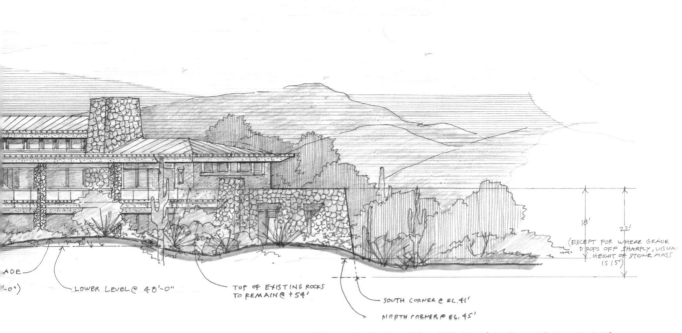

ADE
(-0")

LOWER LEVEL @ 48'-0"

TOP OF EXISTING ROCKS
TO REMAIN @ +54'

SOUTH CORNER @ EL. 41'

NORTH CORNER @ EL. 45'

18'

22'

(EXCEPT FOR WHERE GRADE
DROPS OFF SHARPLY, VISUAL
HEIGHT OF STONE MASS
IS 15')

VIEW FROM THE NORTHWEST

Living in the
mystery of beauty
is performance art
at its best

"The most beautiful thing we can experience is the mysterious. It is the source of all true art and science."
– Albert Einstein

Relatedness and Mystery

Nature is a great teacher. From the open prairies to the oceans, rivers, and streams, and from the vastness of the desert to forests and snow-capped mountains, every landscape radiates both relatedness and variety. Each has its own character and its own truth. Nature's lessons are timeless, and so it should be with the design of our homes.

The physical design of "home" is experienced at four levels, starting with the broadest feelings and continuing to the smallest details. The first is the home's relationship to the natural landscape and to other nearby structures. The second is the human transition between the greater community and one's personal environment. The third is the three-dimensional relationships between interior and exterior space, and the fourth is between the needs of daily life and detailed provisions designed to support all such needs.

At all four levels, nature illustrates the symphonic coherence needed to create a work of art, including relatedness, variety, character, and truth. If design follows nature's example, there will be a feeling of oneness from the driveway approach to the moment of entry, as well as to the experiences of everything within. Instead of confusion, coherent design will lead the eye of the observer. There will be a sense of what is meant to be foreground as opposed to background. When highlighted forms or colors appear, they will be designed to embellish the overall setting. Such accents add delight and excitement, much like walking through the woods and coming upon flame-bright wildflowers against a background of muted grasses, trees, and shrubs.

Like nature itself, a house has changing moods. When well-considered, these moods further the enjoyment of each day and season. The design framework may be established, but like musicians following an orchestral score, the beauty of each moment is still dependent on its level of performance. To live in a dynamically nurturing environment is to enjoy the inspiration of an ever-unfolding experience of what a special place can be.

Connections

Following a benefit concert at my home, I was approached by a man I didn't know who said, "I have a question. This house is full of people, laughing and talking, in fact it is quite noisy, but it is also calm and peaceful, how is that possible?" He was looking for a theory, but my only answer was that architecture can produce a different sense of "quiet" than what can be measured in decibels or easily expressed in words. It is an intangible encounter with the mysterious.

Beyond any clarity of cause and effect, architecture is a spiritual pursuit of connections; connections to the earth, connections to the artistry of human achievement, connections between the timely and the timeless, and maybe even between being in a room full of people, and the ability to feel a personal sense of serenity.

Ancestral Home

Because architectural exploration can awaken our deepest levels of desire, it most often broadens what we believe to be possible. Nowhere are personal feelings more formative than in the design of the spaces and environments in which we live. It is common to look at the accomplishments of antiquity as though they were produced in some manner quite different than how we act today. But when considering the spirit of design, the most ancient of ancestral homes didn't just happen, they were all the conscious creation of somebody. As citizens of the 21st century, we are that "somebody." Our ancestral homes will be the ones we create for ourselves. The power of architecture affords a magical time machine, allowing us to give shape, not only to the future, but in a very real sense, to the past.

The homes we design and build today can be a seamless blend of centuries-old ideas expressed in materials and systems that have never existed until now. Our thoughts and dreams can be woven into an ageless tapestry.

The ability to compress time into a work of art is one of architecture's most enduring gifts. When the spirit of design is at its best, notions about old, new, and modern are replaced with the pursuit of richness, innovation, and timelessness. Instead of focusing on isolated things, imitation, or theory, the essence of home becomes an integrated sense of all that is and all that is yet to be.

Architecture is high-level performance art, requiring relationships that are symphonic. The success of an orchestral performance is measured not only by the brilliance of its individual musicians but by the nuances and artfulness of how everything comes together.

The shared feelings of architect and client are equivalent to the composer's sense of music yet unborn. The drawings and specifications are equivalent to the orchestral score. The score is conducted by the architect. The skills of the artisans and craftspeople are analogous to the experience and talents of the musicians.

Continuing with the analogy, a set of drawings and specifications can no more guarantee a great structure than a musical score can guarantee a great performance. The most brilliant music in written form can result in anything from a mediocre, even painful performance, to one that inspires generations to come. So it is with a structure that has been nurtured to life in the hands of master artisans. It is all far more than mere building.

What is common between a great orchestral performance and the construction of a great house is the odyssey of creation. To build a home or to play a musical instrument requires nothing more than technique, but the spirit of great architecture and great music begins where technique leaves off.

Discovery and Trust

The exploratory design of "home" is a three-dimensional metaphor of a desire for self-discovery and self-trust. It is the rudiments of construction made sacred. To take part in the creation of your own home is to be on a spiritual trail that began in the cave and will continue wherever humanity evolves. It is bestowing a timeless sense of the soul on the methods and materials of today. It is spirit made manifest.

As our communities become more populated and more complex, the quality, character, and sanctity of one's home becomes a more important and personal version of the world. The physical house for our bodies is also the spiritual home for what makes us who we are.

No matter what your religious or philosophic beliefs, after the last words of theology have been spoken, we can but acknowledge that we are all part of a living mystery, an eternal flow, more possible to feel than to explain. If open to the mystery, we may avail ourselves to solutions that are always hidden somewhere beyond the obvious. For those who choose this path, there is no greater playground for our senses than the pursuit and the reality of the homes we create for ourselves.

Marriage of house and site: *A house should be a companion to the beauty of its setting, including the use of color, forms, lighting, landscaping, terraces, and other architectural extensions that marry the house to the land.*

Design Development

Design is a continuous process starting with the broadest generalities and evolving into refinements of the smallest details. The Design Development Phase occurs after the program has been fully established, the plan has been designed, and at least a preliminary selection of all major materials has been made. This is the phase where the following elements are coordinated into a single concept:

1 Room sizes and layouts.
2 Ceiling heights and shapes.
3 Elevations, doors, and window systems.
4 Materials, colors, and finishes.
5 Pool, fountains, terraces, and landscaping.
6 Mechanical and structural systems.
7 All special features.

The exploratory dialogue between architect and client falls into two categories. The easiest to discuss are design aspects that can be reasonably quantified; for example, "The kitchen is this size because ...." More difficult are matters relating to pure design, for example, "Why did you make this room circular?" At this point, there are no rules of engagement other than this useful bit of advice. If the client sees a design element that they want changed, it would be wise for them to first do everything possible to understand why the architect wanted it that way. Conversely, the architect should try to fully understand the request. More often than not, something preferred by both parties will emerge beyond the starting point of either.

Everything up to the Design Development Phase is broadly exploratory. Now is the time for a focused integration of everything stated or implied during the shared exploration. This is where the design comes together into something greater than the sum of its parts.

Path of the Sun: *Because the effect of the sun is different on all sides of a house, provisions for addressing light and shade differ as well, as can be seen in the opposite elevations of the house on the facing page.*

Construction Documents

By way of drawings, specifications, samples, and mock-ups, the design is now translated into a set of bid documents. The list of drawings will typically include something like the following:

1 Civil Site Plan and Notes
2 Architectural Site Plans
3 Foundation Plans
4 Floor Plans
5 Framing Plans
6 Roof and Clerestory Plans
7 Reflected Ceiling Plans
8 Building Sections
9 Fireplace Sections
10 Stairways
11 Wall Sections
12 Exterior Elevations
13 Interior Elevations
14 Door Schedule
15 Window Schedule
16 Finish Schedule
17 Appliance Plans

18 Structural Notes
19 Structural Details
20 Mechanical Details
21 Heating, Ventilating, and Air-Conditioning
22 Plumbing Plans
23 Roof Drainage
24 Electrical Plans
25 Lighting Layouts
26 Electrical and Plumbing Schedules

Plus drawings for all specialty items, including landscaping and irrigation, home theater, interior design, closets, security and control systems.

The total sheet count will vary with the size and complexity of the house; for example, the number of floor plans (item 4) may range from three to ten, with multiple sheets, as required, for the other categories.

Focused Views: *The irregular perimeter of the model to the left takes into account views from the house, and views of the house The house on the facing page is positioned on a high mesa where all the views are downward with no upper landforms or vegetation. By contrast, the house on the following two pages is designed to take advantage of both downhill views as well as those looking up at a mountainside of exotic boulders.*

Truth and Beauty

The poet Yeats' deceptively simple insight that "Beauty is truth, truth is beauty," explains why imitation can never be beautiful. It isn't truthful. It is why the imposition of styles, appropriate to one set of climatic and environmental conditions can never be beautiful in another. Yeats' words describe why wood should be allowed to show its grain, why we love the authentic patina of bronze or copper, why stone should look like stone, and why an exposed natural character is more engaging than making one material look like another.

For two decades, I witnessed visitors touring Frank Lloyd Wright's homes. Visitors came from all parts of the world and from all levels of education. It was fascinating to watch them respond to the magnetism of beauty as truth. Neither Taliesin nor Taliesin West are as "grand" as other places these same visitors have likely toured. There are no crystal chandeliers, no sweeping staircases and no huge rooms. What is evident everywhere is something more rare. It was Wright's vision, integrity, and control that produced these treasured works of art. While touring the buildings and grounds, visitor responses varied from scholarly discourse to a discernible tear in the eye of someone who may have asked no questions. It is at such moments that the viewer gives evidence of what truth and beauty are all about.

At its best, architecture blends structure, materials, form, and space with the surrounding environment to create theater-like settings for the activities of residents and guests. Simplicity feels more genuine, thus more real. The magic of design is to create grandeur without exaggeration, greatness without pretense, and warmth without imitating the past. We are spiritual beings occupying a physical earth. The art of architecture exists to connect our deepest wishes, prayers, and feelings with the environments we call home.

A Poetic Place: *The upper courtyard at Frank Lloyd Wright's Taliesin in Wisconsin.*

Artful living
by way of design
is the highest
form of luxury

5

*"I found early in life that I could get along
without the necessities—if only
I could have the luxuries."*
– Frank Lloyd Wright

Luxury as Necessity

On more than one occasion, I watched Frank Lloyd Wright say things, with a twinkle in his eye, that others would treat as witty while missing the greater truth. A good example is his oft-quoted remark at the top of this page. He wasn't trying to be funny—he meant what he said, and lived it to the hilt. His notion of luxury was not something superfluous or indulgent, but rather a level of artfulness required to live fully.

As soon as we master the pragmatic, there is a human tendency to turn our new "needs" into something creative. We no longer "need" older buildings that have outlived their original usefulness, but by way of historic restoration, we cherish and give heightened meaning to their existence. We no longer need moats for defensive barriers but we need reflecting ponds, pools, cascades, and fountains all the more. We no longer need fireplaces for heat, nor candles for light, but the deeper needs of our soul call out for these primitive uses of fire. While we couldn't exist without food, our diet and places for dining have become more about ritual and celebration than anything to do with survival.

Yearning for the Natural

We can now produce miracles of synthetic fabrics, technologically "improved" lighting, more effective air-conditioning, and plastics that imitate other materials for less cost. At the same time, our desire has never been greater for natural fibers, leathers, daylighting, fresh air, and the richest varieties of natural materials, including wood, stone, metal, adobe, and rammed earth.

The ancients used incense and other fragrances to mask undesirable odors. We now introduce aromas into settings of perfectly fresh air simply to arouse pleasurable sensations. At a time when chemistry can reproduce scents on demand, we desire the smell of natural materials, fresh fruits, and wildflowers. Spices, once necessary for preservation, are now used to enhance the pleasure of taste. Deeply programmed within us are needs and desires that cycle back to the primitive, but always on a higher plane. This evolving process is the artfulness of life.

As we learn more about the sensual needs and healing responses of our bodies, what were once deemed luxuries become necessities. Specialists in all areas are recognizing the therapeutic effects of soothing sounds, aromas, and the healing qualities of water, lotions, and touch. Care for our precious eyesight requires proper lighting and glare-free spaces. Our bodies respond to forms and colors that arouse sensations of wellness, passion, and delight. The more we learn about human sensitivities, the distinction between necessities and luxuries begins to blur.

Fragrance and Touch

Incense and aromatic oils have been used for centuries for both health and enjoyment. Whole industries are dedicated to marketing bottled fragrances to improve our lives when applied to our bodies. Shouldn't the aromas of our homes be at least as important?

In theater design we know that being able to hear well is related to how well we are able to see. In dining, we know that what we smell relates to what we are able to taste.

Urban environments overburden our senses in ways that are neither pleasing nor healthful. Home is where we can restore the balance. Selected species of woods, hides of leather, natural fibers, flowers, and food can add to our sensual delight. Natural and night lighting can be designed to turn our homes into places of theatrical mystery and surprise. And to walk barefoot across polished concrete or stone, wide-planked boards, and a variety of rugs is to enjoy tactile sensations from the ground up.

We too easily deny ourselves the richer qualities of environment that could be basic to our daily experience. Architecture is all about feeling the intangibles. Does the design of the house allow for the warmth of sunlit patterns to play across a variety of materials? Is there an orchestration of well-proportioned space? Does the design include the cooling effect of water and the glare-free diffusion of both natural and night lighting? Is there an interplay between interior and exterior vistas? Does the design provide idealized settings to nurture the needs of work, study, and relaxation?

Fireplaces, along with materials like wood and leather can mean as much to our olfactory senses as they do to sight, warmth, and touch. In his 1943 autobiography, Frank Lloyd Wright included a section called "Sniff Taliesin." Listen as he describes the blessing of scent in his Wisconsin home:

"Taliesin is pervaded by its own very special smell. The visitor on coming in for the first time will sniff and remark upon it, ask what the fragrance is. In Spring and Summer the windows are thrown wide-open. The odor of the long white drifts of wild-plum blooming on the nearby hillsides drifts in—the crabapple and hawthorn in the meadows send their scent on over the treetops... In Autumn, mingling with the odor of freshly burned oak, is the smell of bowls of apples and unshelled shag-bark hickory nuts—the prince of all perfumes. But for the Winter, there inside the rooms is newly gathered, everlasting, cream-white antimony. This gentle pervading odor of antimony is to the sense of smell what the flavor of slippery elm is to the young boy's sense of taste. Oak fires then start in the seventeen ever-present stone fireplaces ... The tang of burned oak and the strange odor of antimony together in fresh air—this is the authentic recipe for "the Taliesin Smell."

Sensory Pleasure: *Interior spaces are far more than places to put "things." They are also a playground for the scents of fresh bread, fruit, flowers, and natural fibers. Purely functional elements can be made to feel rich with the touch of stone, tile, wood, granite, polished steel countertops, decorative metal wall-facings, and a curving deerskin handrail. Lighting is a basic need, but it can also be designed to add mystery and a glowing patina across an array of rich warm materials.*

Enriching Space: *The fireplace and furnishings to the right define an intimate seating area, made more interesting by the space that continues past both sides of the fireplace. In the top photo, artwork is framed with columned shapes and corresponding sky-lit ceiling forms. The colors of the master suite are enriched with geometric patterns and textures.*

Permitting and Bidding

Some approvals are secured during the design stage. Examples include steep sites governed by a municipal hillside ordinance, applying for variances, and presenting preliminary drawings for design review to a homeowners association.

When the drawings and specifications are completed, the selected contractor will put them out for competitive subcontractor bids to firms that are well-established and preferably those having a successful record of prior work with the general contractor.

Itemized bids will be reviewed by the contractor, and where helpful, by the architect. Anything that appears out of line should be re-bid until the pricing matches the work product. This is not always a matter of lowering the bid. A bid amount that appears unexpectedly low should be analyzed as carefully as one that appears too high. There is no merit in entering into a contract with someone who has made a mistake and will never make it to the finish line.

To conserve time, the bidding period is often conducted simultaneously with the time required to process a city building permit. If the property is part of a homeowners association, the architectural review process may require a final review of the completed documents.

Capturing Views: *Nothing does more to create excitement on any given site than to frame views that did not appear to exist without the architecture. The above view of the hillside was created by a series of stepped retaining walls, terraced into the mountain. Tall, butt-glazed windows were used to open the room to the uphill slope and sky beyond. The house on the facing page was designed to frame views of its foreground golf course.*

Sensuality combines our primitive need for shelter with our spiritual need for celebration

*"The best places always make you
feel like all is well with the world."*
– Andrei Codrescu

Sensual Spaces

Think of all the places where you have felt pleasurable impressions. Some are dark and mysterious, others sun-drenched, some may be monastery-like in their simplicity, while still others are richly ornamented and colorful. Some memorable places are quiet, others filled with music and movement, or distinguished by exotic aromas. The places we remember have natural breezes rather than hermetically sealed, recirculated air. They have soft lighting rather than harsh, hot spots, or flickering fluorescents. When we listen to the sounds of birds or watch the movement of trees, or the shimmering light on water, we somehow feel more healthy, more alive, more in tune with the sustaining beauty of nature.

We travel hundreds and thousands of miles to experience optimally sensual places for only brief periods before returning to "reality." That this is regrettable is obvious. Unless our homes can provide these qualities, it matters little how large the rooms are, how high the ceilings are, or how expensive the appliances and furnishings may be. Sensuality is a basic need for a fulfilling life, and is best when the experience is as natural as we can make it. The need for natural breezes, the sights and sounds of nature, and the ever-changing play of light and shade will always be the soul of any memorably timeless experience.

When what we remember is limited to what we think and say, that is the least part of what we are all about. Life at its finest demands more than thoughts and words. That is why we have music, painting, and dance. Feel the passion in the flamencan dancer to sense something that words could never express. The spirit of architecture is to building what a Beethoven symphony is to noise.

All the money in the world could not possibly produce the works of Beethoven or any other great artist. Such works represent the wealth of our humanness.

Impressions of architecture cannot be described solely in terms of materials and dimensions. High ceilings are fine, but the feeling of spaciousness is far more convincing when it results from an artful relativity of heights rather than needlessly exaggerated dimensions. No matter how large the house, there should be small, cozy spaces. It has been said that no one has ever had a great idea in a big room.

The Words We Use

I once asked a group of advanced architectural students to consider the design of a house, avoiding all references to commonly used room names. The assignment provoked creative ways to think about the essence of home rather than falling back on justifications for shapes and sizes that spring to mind when using familiar words like *living room, bedroom, bathroom,* or *kitchen.*

The process of design is restricted or liberated by the words we use in other ways as well. When a person says, "I want a Spanish Colonial or Mediterranean Southwest design," neither architect nor client could possibly know what that means, other than that the words serve to thwart a more genuine exploration. Someone once asked the great architect, Louis Kahn, to design a colonial house. He explained that he did not do colonial houses, whereupon his potential client asked if he could recommend someone who did. "Sure," Kahn responded, "Thomas Jefferson, but he's been dead for more than 200 years."

Light and Air

Human response to the natural environment is complex. If it were not so, the finest architectural experience could be achieved by simply sitting outside in beautiful settings. In fact, we require controlled separation from the natural beauty we admire. Our feelings about light and air are complicated. The sun can cause us to suffer skin cancer and light can fade the contents of our homes. A little movement of air is pleasant, but too much is one of nature's most harassing elements, or as Frank Lloyd Wright called them, the "hellements." It is not only rain that we need to be sheltered from, even without rain, if a terrace or patio does not have some covering, it will seldom be used.

Trellises can be used for transition from the intensity of exposure under the sky to relatively darker interiors. These same trellises can be positioned to "paint" ever-changing patterns of light and shade from the sun by day and garden lighting at night.

Natural light is best when bounced from surface to surface, allowing it to be indirect and free of glare. Wherever possible, windows should be placed to allow light to enter all spaces from two or more directions. Clerestory windows and other forms of "scoops" can be used to capture light from directions where there are no windows.

Slotted windows, light shelves, grilles, overhangs, and deep side recesses are all architectural devices for moderating and directing the character and quality of sunlight. Forms that are too boxy tend to appear lifeless, with or without the sun. Where shapes have been sculpted with clear intent, the ever-changing patterns of moving light are a gift of nature.

Many places enjoy cooler night air, yet one can walk through neighborhoods on a cool evening, listening to refrigeration units whirring away as though it were high noon. For reasons of security or allergic reaction to pollens, people may not wish to keep their windows open throughout the night, but there are other ways to achieve the benefits of natural ventilation.

In addition to good insulation, most modern houses lack the thermal mass to store up the coolness of night and heat from the day. In warm climates, 75 percent of all energy use goes for refrigeration, thus the greatest savings are those that result from decreasing the amount of time that refrigerated air is used. Fractional horsepower fans can draw in filtered air to be further distributed by ceiling fans, all pulled and exhausted by way of whole-house ventilators. It obviously helps if the overall design is conceived with this natural flow in mind.

We are only now beginning to design for the benefits of doing more with less, more daylighting with less consumption of electricity, more natural air with less need for refrigeration and stale air. And while the technological efficiency of household equipment is improving, conservation will remain mainly behavioral and the issue is circular. More conservational behavior permits more opportunities for designed efficiencies, which in turn can take greater advantage of behavioral patterns. It is a matter of working with nature rather than against it. The payoff for being in tune with the elements is only partly measured in kilowatts. It is also an exposure to the healing sense of natural light and air that can be experienced no other way.

Designing with Light: *The ever-changing play of light and shade adds a richness to form. The patterns from the sun can be augmented with up-lighting at night to project similar patterns in the opposite direction.*

"Light, God's eldest daughter,
is a principal element of beauty."
– Thomas Fuller

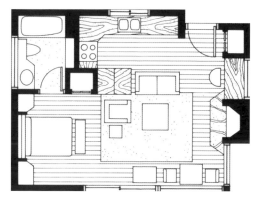

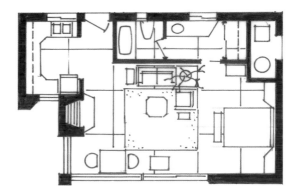

Detailed Variety: *Clerestory windows by day and indirect lighting by night have been designed to bathe the interiors with changing patterns of illumination. In a single open space, these two guest houses provide cozy areas for the bed, a sitting area, game table, and kitchen. Ceiling treatments are used to differentiate the sleeping from the living areas. Only the bathrooms are treated as separate spaces. While almost identical in plan, slight adjustments make these two guest houses feel like very different places.*

Bathrooms: *Large or small, bathroom spaces should have a sense of magic, convenience, and intimacy. Bathrooms are places for mirrors, dimmable lighting, flowers, and for some people, more candles than anywhere else in the house.*

94

Utility and Warmth: *Both bathrooms and kitchens are best when designed to combine a laboratory-like clarity with the warmth and elegance of the rest of the house. The examples show the use of a variety of materials, including metals, wood, granite, glass, and tile.*

Multi-use Places: *When the focus of design is on human use and comfort rather than preconceived notions about function or style, all rooms become "living rooms." Gathering places occur throughout connecting spaces, with their varied character adding color and richness to the diversity of daily living.*

The Entry Experience: *Mahogany gates lead to a curving path along a natural arc of giant boulders. A slightly rising bridge crosses an entry pond before arriving at a stone arch and carved mahogany door beyond. Once inside, the interior space opens out to a foreground view of terraces, pools, and fountains, and to a background horizon of distant mountains.*

Home as Theater

Early in the design phase, one of our clients insisted that he wanted his guests be able to drive up to a front door clearly in evidence for all to see. Given the constraints of his site, but more importantly the opportunities, this requirement did not seem to be in our client's best interest, yet he persisted. Our only hope was to be uncommonly convincing that his front door would be best if it could be more "discovered" than anything too obvious.

The site was a breathtakingly beautiful, five-acre hillside with a backdrop of huge, other worldly boulders, all in an exclusive gated community. The area selected for the house occurred 2,000 feet from the end of a private street. Because the landforms and vegetation had a mystical beauty, we challenged our client by posing this question. *"How is it possible to add something to your property which has a planned overall footprint of approximately 14,000 square feet plus the entrance drive, in a way that accomplishes everything in your program while preserving the mystery and majesty of the land?"*

We assured our client that if he would let us decide how to treat the location of the entry, we would offer the following answer: *"In the time and space between parking their cars and approaching the front door, your guests will transition from the anxious world of the street, to the timeless mystery of the land. The design of your home will cut with knife-like precision through its richly varied topography. You and your guests will enjoy optimal comfort, solar angles and views, as well as the natural beauty and primitive characteristics of the site. In the finest tradition of architecture, you will experience the natural setting, uncompromised and made more dramatic by the presence of what you have built."*

We proposed a design that occurred on seven levels and extended longer than the length of a football field. We asked our client to reconsider the whole idea as to what constitutes a "front door." Because he wanted the experience to have a certain drama, we used the analogy of going to the theater. We asked him to consider that turning off the city street and passing through the gated entry to his community was equivalent to arriving at the outer lobby. Winding up the curvilinear drive to the house was equivalent to entering the theater itself. And as his guests walked through the garden gates, this was equivalent to the orchestral prelude. And finally, as the 12-foot high entry door swung open, it would be analogous to the breath-taking flourish of the curtain going up ... show time! Happily, the imagery was convincing and the house and entrance were built accordingly.

Like the theater, a good house becomes a place where life is played out with artful expression. Beyond the reach of the theater, the atmosphere of "home" is enlivened by the changing moods of morning, noon, and night and by the atmospheric effects of the seasons. A great house intensifies the beauty in these changes, making the occupants more aware of their surroundings, thus more alive. All truly great houses express the aspirations of their owners and then go on to become a sustaining influence in furthering who they are. Winston Churchill's oft-quoted testimony to this truth is "First we shape our environments, then they shape us."

Dressed For Dinner

Like their human counterparts, good houses are capable of a host of moods to make them more interesting. This happens throughout the year in response to the changing seasons, and each day as sunlight from above gives way to architectural lighting from within.

Forms, spaces, and the transparency of glass become a three-dimensional framework on which to project whatever character is most supportive for the desired mood. The changing character of lighting can provide the proper setting for everything from a blues ensemble to a string quartet. Strategic lighting sets the stage for each event, no less so in a good home than for good theater.

The gift of
an enduring design is
to always feel that
you've come home
to a special place

*"The dreams which accompany all
human actions should be nurtured
by the places in which people live."*
– Charles W. Moore

The Celebration of Place

When my two daughters were very little, the event of going to bed was accompanied by a careful placement of stuffed animals, extra pillows, and favorite blankets. I have come to see this cozy, childhood nest-making as an early version of environmental design.

The urge to design for others is an extension of my own unquenchable desire to live, work, and play in beautiful surroundings. When growing up in Chicago, my favorite play area was the only square block near my home that had not yet been developed. We called it "The Prairie." In contrast to the dreariness of its urban surroundings, this untouched patch of Midwestern landscape was covered with wildflowers, weeds, and native grasses. It was my private wilderness—a place of fantasy and dreams. I could disappear into the silence of the subtle colors and scents of nature, feeling emboldened by the protection that my "prairie home" provided from the rest of the world.

Living in a Tent

Two months before my 18th birthday, whatever special places I had experienced or imagined while living in Chicago exploded into the mysterious atmosphere of Taliesin West in Arizona. Instead of being surrounded by dense urban development, I was now immersed in the exotic vastness of the Sonoran desert with no development in sight. On my second day as Frank Lloyd Wright's youngest apprentice, I was given a bucket of mortar and taken out to a partially completed tent. After brief instructions as to how to finish what someone else had started, I was told that the tent would be my new home.

By way of published articles and television accounts, many people know that Wright's apprentices slept in tents, but few know the life-changing depth of that experience. Unless you have been a desert nomad, you probably don't know what it feels like to go "home," night after night, by walking out into a horizon-to-horizon embrace of starlight against the pitch black canopy of night.

My little "home" had a recessed concrete floor surrounded by stone walls. It had a colored concrete terrace with an outdoor firepit. Reddish brown, pyramid-shaped fabric was stretched over steel supports with zippers in the center of two triangular sides. One side faced the terrace and the other looked out to a deep wash below. The tent was most often left open with its canvas flaps folded back, making triangular portals in both directions.

The floor was covered with padding and a red rug, both fitting tightly against stone walls. Brightly colored pillows were placed against three of the walls, with the fourth opening out to broad steps up to a terrace. Candles, lanterns, and torches were everywhere. The softness of the fabric, the earthiness of the stone, and the primitive use of fire made everything feel more like the Arabian Knights than anything to do with camping out.

Living in direct exposure to nature allowed me to practice on myself. My tent "home" was an encounter with the fundamentals of form, space, light, air, and comfort—the very same variables that are critical in the design of homes from the smallest to the most grand.

The Studio

In the more than two decades since leaving the Wright organization and designing for others, I've been privileged to create a trilogy of places for myself. The first was The Studio, a custom "home," but of another kind. It may seem strange to discuss my workplace in a book dedicated to the design of custom homes, especially given our society's tendency to make a complete separation between home and work. For a growing number of people, that separation is no longer desired.

While we lavish attention on our primary residences, many people still accept that their office environments can get along with inoperable windows, acoustical tile ceilings, look-alike lobbies, spaces that are more hygienic than inspiring, and long corridors that are anything but warm and friendly. Considering how much of our waking hours are spent in places of work, it is tragic that they aren't designed to nurture the same human values that are considered in a good house. When my wife picks me up for lunch and afterward I ask her to drop me off "at home," we both know that means The Studio.

In the fall of 1996, we had an early morning visit at The Studio from Dr. Mohammed Alsheik, the then Minister of Municipal and Rural Affairs for Saudi Arabia. After a brief greeting, Dr. Mohammed said, "I experienced something upon my arrival that I'd like to share." He went on to say, "I can imagine one of your clients driving up in haste, preoccupied with his problems and possibly even upset about something to do with what you had designed." I worried about where this story would lead. Dr. Mohammed continued, "As your client gets out of his car and moves toward the portal gates, the walk rises slightly which slows him down just a bit. He enters past the great mahogany doors but instead of being inside, he finds that he has entered a garden courtyard surrounded by the sights and sounds of hummingbirds, flowing water, and the subtle fragrance of flowering vegetation.

He continues along a curving walk, coming under the shelter of the canopied entry. As he opens the door, he is now looking straight through the lobby into another sun-lit garden beyond. Two sets of clerestory windows filter natural light through hanging plants and he is greeted on both sides by gracious receptionists. As he looks around, open passages extend in all directions, and he sees walls ornamented with the words of Oscar Wilde, William James, and others. By the time he's ushered into your office his feelings of hurry and anger have dissipated—he is now at home and in a more thoughtful state of mind."

Many people have commented on our Studio environment, but none so poetic as this visitor from the Middle East. That the experience of walking from one's car to the entry of an office building can produce such an impression is confirmation of the power of place.

The Studio Setting: *Located on a major thoroughfare in the heart of the city, The Studio complex is barely visible from the street. Just a few steps from the urban environment, there is a sense of wildness. Portal entry gates lead into a cascading water garden, surrounded with the colors and fragrances of indigenous plantings. Once inside the courtyard, another pair of entry doors opens into a lobby, that leads out to a second walled garden beyond.*

107

Karakahl

The second in my trilogy of homes is a carpenter-crafted, country place on the Mogollon Rim in northeast Arizona. The sloping site overlooks a clearing framed by Ponderosa pines, some of which are 200 years old. The wooded setting inspired a decentralized complex, including the main house, a treehouse and play area, a stone and timber firepit, and a separate studio with an attached carport and small garage for storing winter toys.

Karakahl is a Norwegian word meaning a place of health, healing, and care. It is located on a sloping site overlooking a meadow on the edge of a 200,000 acre national forest. While the structures were lovingly designed and crafted, what makes Karakahl special is not so much its roof and walls, but the way in which it intensifies the character of the surrounding environment.

Our guest book chronicles this special sense felt by those who come to visit. The compound seems to heighten a playfulness that comes from being in the forest. Upon arrival, our young daughters and their guests would frequently launch into planning plays and dances that they performed without prompting from the adults.

The forest character weaves in and around the complex and every opportunity has been taken to frame views while flooding the interiors with natural light. The landscaping approach has been simply to restore the forest floor. Arizona fescue and wildflowers are the connecting tissue between the structures and the surrounding stand of pine trees. While there are no lawns or formal gardens, large concrete bowls are filled with spreading junipers. At 7,700 feet above sea level, there are heavy summer rains and winter snowfalls. Steep metal roofs shed snow and the geometry of the design directs all drifts away from windows and doors.

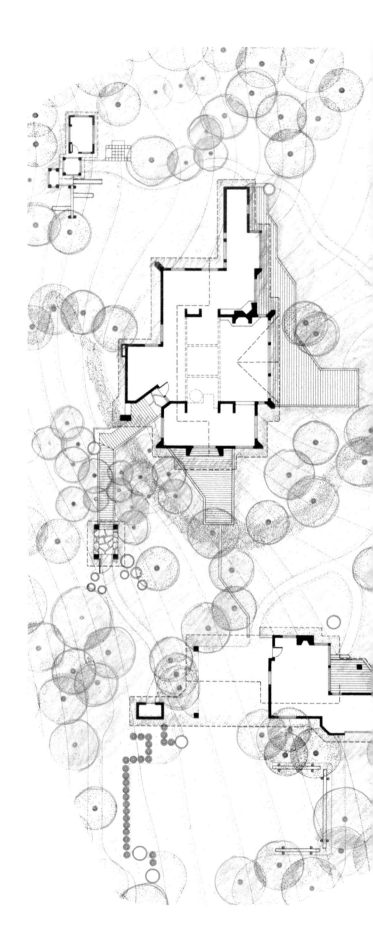

Entering the Compound: *A carport and studio serve as the entry point to the main house. Clerestory windows can be seen into the studio to the right. Similar windows occur in the distance on the main house, to the left.*

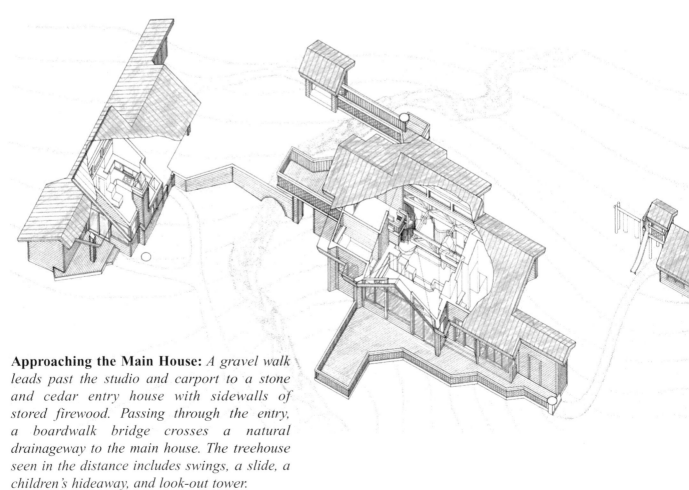

Approaching the Main House: *A gravel walk leads past the studio and carport to a stone and cedar entry house with sidewalls of stored firewood. Passing through the entry, a boardwalk bridge crosses a natural drainageway to the main house. The treehouse seen in the distance includes swings, a slide, a children's hideaway, and look-out tower.*

*"The art of architecture studies not structure in itself,
but the effect of structure
on the human spirit."*
– Geoffrey Scott

Designed for all Seasons: *It is great fun to experience a house change its personality with each season, being open and airy for summer, and cozy and sheltering during the winter. Karakahl's main central space is shown on the following two pages.*

Skyfire

My family's principal residence was designed for a gently sloping site in the Sonoran desert. My wife and I began by searching for a core idea to inspire the design. We asked ourselves, "If we were to design a true desert house, imitating neither styles from elsewhere nor the prevailing desert favorites of Santa Fe, Santa Barbara, or Spanish Colonial, what would that be?" One of the more obvious parts to the answer was that it would have to represent a convincing bond with its setting.

The name Skyfire was selected to symbolize an ongoing dialogue with the atmospheric beauty of the desert. The design became an unfolding layering of experiences, each as preparation for the next. A pair of ornamental steel gates opens to a narrow earthen drive with desert landscaping on both sides. The drive crosses under a timber frame with a hanging steel entry sign, reminiscent of the ranches that once populated the area. A desert path leads up to a pair of steel-brushed mahogany board doors with ornamental, blacksmith-forged hardware. There are no sidelights and no hint from the outside as to what occurs beyond the doors. Vegetation crowds in on both sides of the entrance path while a low-ceilinged entryway compresses the moment as preparation for what follows.

As the entry door swings open, the view is through the living room, across a reflecting pool and out to a horizon of mountains some 50 miles away. While this same view existed along the roadway up to the house, the difference is that the entry procession dramatizes the experience just as the musical prelude and proscenium arch in a theater setting are used to position and dramatize the action on stage. Skyfire's materials include colored concrete, exposed wood, copper and steel (both left to patina naturally), and the use of sweeping canvas canopies.

Once the design was finalized and the drawings and details completed, Skyfire took nearly two years to build. During that time my family and I lived comfortably in a rental house less than half the size of what was to become our new home. As the time approached to move, we felt none of the expected excitement associated with getting a larger house with everything being new. What we did feel was that our new environment would change us in positive ways. In addition to the search for a true desert expression, our home had been designed with personal and family questions in mind; "Who are we as a family?" "What do we value?" and "What do we wish to celebrate?" The answers to these eternal human questions, expressed in three-dimensional structures, spaces, and gardens, are far more compelling than any of the easier — to-achieve notions of bigness, newness, or luxury. The most gratifying achievements are undefinably spiritual.

Like the cozy placement of children's blankets, toys, and pillows, referred to at the beginning of this chapter, architecture should inspire a protective, familiar feeling, as well as some degree of interaction with the larger setting. Architectural features, both large and small, can be used to define courtyards and places of passage. Decentralized elements can be arranged using free-standing trellises, wing walls, fences, and landscaping as a bond between nature and the built environment.

Designs that inspire a genuine interplay between architecture and one's deepest feelings are a forever mystery, never revealing the whole story, and offering something to engage the imaginations of those who come in contact with the space. A good home is like a good friend — always there for you and always offering support, surprise, and delight.

Skyfire and its Environs: *The compound includes a gated driveway, detached desert cottage, an upper level exercise loft, and viewing deck. Natural materials include thick concrete walls, tinted concrete and wood plank floors, board walls and ceilings, exposed steel, fabric canopies, and copper roofs.*

120

The Hidden Entry: *The drawing to the right shows a pair of entry doors, but add the effect of the sun and the reality of the entry becomes far more cave-like. Curved, sloping walls, meandering landscaping, and filtered light through an overhead trellis, all welcome arriving guests to a bit of mystery. In just a few steps, a transition is felt between the harsh exposure of the desert sky to sheltering views of the valley below.*

Fabric Architecture: *A world of possibilities exists beyond the more limited use of the traditional awning. The guest house on the facing page has a character shaped more by the design of its terrace canopy than the structure itself. The free-standing shelter above, echoes the forms of a stylized nomadic tent. Stretched fabric forms, along with the garden and fireplace, provide a place for reflection and intimate conversations.*

Personality and Style

Every good house has its own personality. No matter how many elements have been mixed together, the overall design has a feeling of being certain of itself. Authentic character is an affair of the heart. It begins with each new client stimulating the imagination of the architect. For the creative designer, no matter how many times he or she has gone through the process, each relationship is unique and, at its best, thrilling.

Simple Forms: *Integrally colored venetian finishes are used, both inside and out, to reflect the same multi-toned depth as its centuries-old European counterparts. A palette of colors was derived from the burnished hues of the desert.*

Intriguing places
like interesting people
are always in the
process of
becoming

The Living Home

We enjoy looking at photographs of beautiful houses, furnishings, and gardens. No less enjoyable is to try and imagine the unfolding life to be lived within these varied settings. Achieving a richer life is the true objective when designing a custom home.

Very early in my career, I was privileged to serve as project architect for an 1,800-seat theater in Sarasota, Florida. After years of designing, detailing, fighting to get the building costs within budget, and ultimately overseeing construction, the structure was finished, but that was only the beginning of the life that had been created. Opening night was "Fiddler on the Roof," followed on the second night by "Man of La Mancha." There have been nearly three decades of successful performances since, but I will never forget those first two nights. On both occasions, I stood crying my eyes out as I watched, what had been a construction project, begin to take on a life of its own as a living, breathing feature of peoples lives. I have had that feeling again and again as words shared with a client evolve into drawings, then a construction site and ultimately a home environment that transcends any hoped-for achievement in the steps along the way.

The most rewarding designs are never "finished." The acquisition of new artwork, new furnishings and accessories, fresh flowers, a growing landscape, along with the patina of time, continue to inspire new impressions from owners and guests alike.

The changing moods of "home" can be that of a resort, a theater, or a gallery displaying the artifacts of life, some timely, some timeless. Towels, bed linens, bowls of fruit, flowers, fixtures, and appliances are timely. Paintings, sculpture, furniture, rugs, patterned glass, candle holders, lighting fixtures, and tableware are all more timeless. As much as possible, both the timely and the timeless should be works of art.

Because of my feelings about what a house can be, I have often pondered what it means when we speak of a "work of art." In addition to sculptors, painters, dancers, musicians, architects, and writers, might we not apply the term "artist" to a broader range of participants? The desire to define artist in a more inclusive sense is to acknowledge that art is a quality of the spirit, not limited by any medium of expression. What constitutes "art," as displayed in the architectural gallery of one's home, is that it has a spiritual bond of belonging to the character of the house, in the same way that the spirit of the overall house belongs to the character of its setting.

When design is genuine, everything appears more timeless than new. While systems, fixtures, and appliances are best when new, the house itself along with all artifacts, displayed or used within, should feel too natural to be thought of as being either new or old.

Furnishings and Accessories

Architecture is most exciting when a clear direction can be felt, starting with the land and continuing throughout the house including all interior finishes and artifacts. The notion of "taste" is giving way to how well furnishings actually perform, both functionally and spiritually. Unless there is an underlying concept to direct the selections, homes filled with even the finest furnishings can appear to be nothing more than mini-versions of the showrooms from which the items were purchased. A showroom is a place for a wide array of choices but in a home these choices must speak as a coherent idea.

Life-enriching furnishings include musical instruments, to be played by family members and guests, shelves of books, that someone either has read or intends to read, office and kitchen areas that are beautifully designed with laboratory-like clarity. Paintings, pottery, sculpture, lacquer boxes, and other items collected for their intrinsic beauty should be used to further animate all spaces. Everything is more valued if it somehow plays a part in the overall story. It matters little whether you have a Louis XIV chair or Marie-Antoinette's creamer, modest or grand, furnishings are only so many "things" until they become features of a greater idea.

"Making the simple complicated is commonplace; making the complicated simple, awesomely simple, that's creativity."
– Charles Mingus

Simplicity is not simple: *Even in the earliest stages of design, when working to fit the owners' program within the constraints of the site, there must be a feeling for the finished work. It is what Frank Lloyd Wright called, "Having a sense of the as-yet-unborn whole in mind." In the above photo, a gentle curve in plan, was conceived as a gallery, with overhead skylights by day, and lighting from below to illuminate glass sculpture that did not exist at the time but was anticipated by the initial design. The idea of the plan becomes a framework that heightens the meaning of everything to follow.*

A Trio of Tables: *Designed to facilitate a grouping of furnishings in an open and curving space, these three geometric tables are as natural in their setting as rectangular forms would be in a rectangular room. The inlaid dining table shown to the left and on the facing page is curved at the same radius as the house itself.*

"Architecture is inhabited sculpture." – Constantin Brancusi

Custom Millwork: *A triangular table forms the organizing element for a seating group facing the sit-down bar. The painting over the bar is motorized to conceal a large-screen television. Three panels over the back bar open to storage areas for beverage accessories. The center panel is shown in the open position. An adjacent storage room is entered through a pivoting section of the built-in bookshelves. The interior on the facing page shows the design continuity of the circular character carried into stone countertops, moldings and ceiling shapes. It is also expressed in concentric stone patterns in the floor.*

California Poppies: *The top photo is the flower, the middle, the abstraction and the bottom is a mural executed on mahogany with stain, oil paint, and gold leaf.*

Nature Pattern

The most notable periods of architecture have found expression in a close relationship between created space and ornamentation. Historic examples include the Parthenon, Chartres Cathedral, and the Pazzi Chapel of Renaissance architect Filippo Brunelleschi. Whether looking at the rose windows of the Gothic cathedrals or the fluted columns of the ancient Greeks, the inspiration for ornamentation has always owed much to the patterns and sensations experienced in nature.

In the 20th century, the genius of Frank Lloyd Wright gave new life to the marriage of art and architecture, especially in its application to the custom home. His murals, tapestries, and carpet patterns have been displayed around the world and are valued features of the Metropolitan Museum's collection of American art.

The study of nature was Wright's constant companion and his source for continually fresh pattern and structure. His method of looking at nature in an abstract sense was designed to increase his vocabulary for pattern, with the same advantage that an increased vocabulary of words benefit a writer or speaker.

The abstracted nature pattern studies shown on these two pages have been utilized to create everything from the geometry of complex plan shapes to specialty items for interior artifacts shown on the following pages. The richness of integral ornamentation is the design of artwork conceived for a specific place. Walls, ceilings, floors, and windows are all candidates for the imagination, including sculpture, murals, lighting, fountains, art glass, wall hangings, linens, tableware, rugs, and innovative versions of the traditional fireplace.

"Method in creation will come freely to him who learns to see in the abstract. Study the geometry that is the idea of every form. Learn the essential pattern that makes the oak and distinguishes it from the pattern that makes the pine. Try after this, the curling vine, and flowing water. Then try the flowers. A chrysanthemum is easy, a rock or rose is difficult. Try this method and gradually discipline your power to see. Get patiently to the point where you naturally see this element of pattern in everything."

– Frank Lloyd Wright

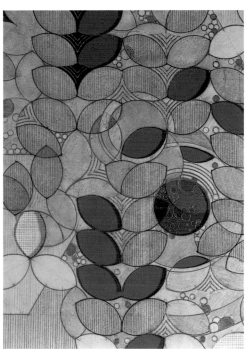

Integral Artwork

We are frequently asked to accommodate specific sculpture or paintings. When the client is a collector we do a capacity analysis to indicate how their collection and its future growth might be accommodated.

Our plans also explore opportunities for special features; for example, custom rugs, murals, lighting, or sculpture that the client may either find or commission for the space.

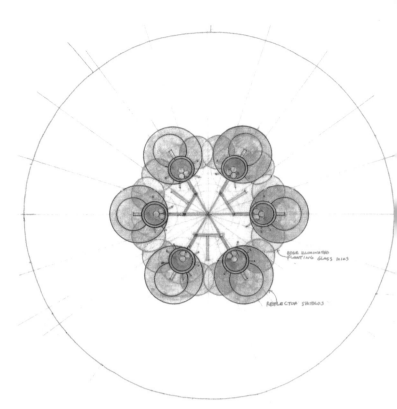

For a house with a circular entry, we suggested that there be a piece of sculpture that could be seen from three levels. Five years after the owners moved in they returned to ask if we would create a pendant sculpture in response to our original suggestion. The result is shown to the right. At the top is the original drawing, the middle photo is the sculpture being installed, and the bottom photo is looking up from below after completion. Called "Sonoran Stalactites," the aluminum and glass forms are internally illuminated and suspended from a single anchor that had been provided in the original construction. The drawing below is a venetian plaster and mahogany-trim, ceiling-design for a circular room in the same house.

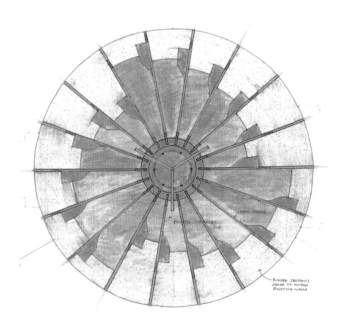

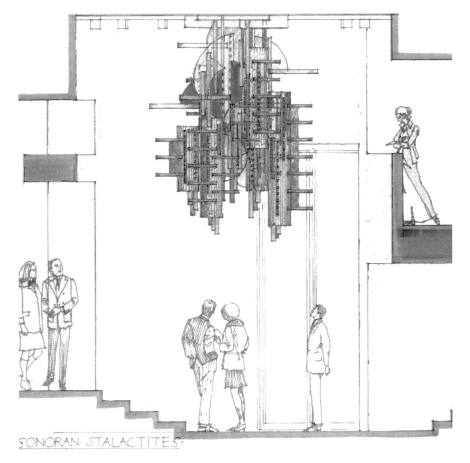

SONORAN STALACTITES·

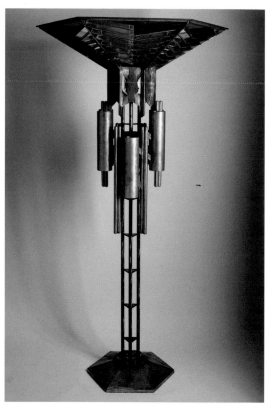

Relatedness and Scale

One of the most compelling reasons to commission pieces for special spaces, for example, a floor lamp that might otherwise be simply purchased, is to create more suitable relationships to the scale and character of the space of which it is a feature. That was the motivation for the custom design of the free-standing lamp shown on this page and in its setting on the facing page. A wooden study model and the lamp prior to receiving its blackened finish are shown above.

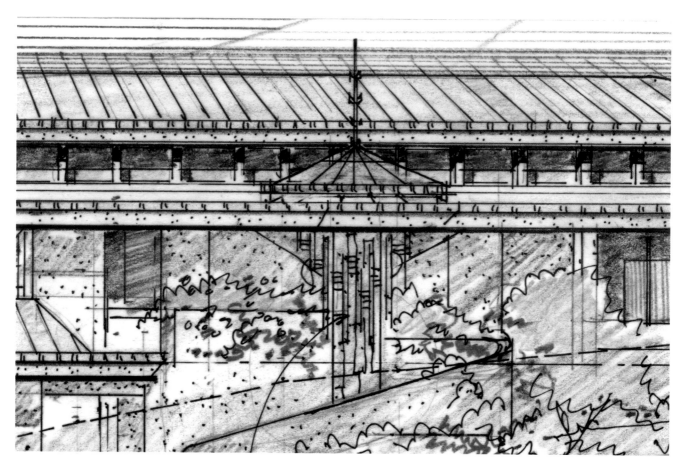

150

Saguaro Forest Sculpture

Designed to animate the stone approach to an upper level entry, the work consists of a 10-foot diameter skylight over a series of colorful steel tubes. Playing off the soft lavender hues of the desert, the skylight filters light across the shapes by day while internal lighting creates a glowing pattern of light and shade by night. The skylight form can be seen in the conceptual sketch at the top of the facing page and below left is a wooden study model. The sculpture consists of 56 cylinders which range from 18 inches to five feet in length.

Interlocking Squares: *Three color patterns of the design are shown with the completed rug above.*

Clockwise from upper left: *1) A pair of 36 inch custom door pulls of forged iron and brass; 2) Ornamental bronze, overhead garage doors; 3) Mahogany entry door and side lights; 4) Bronze plant stand with integral lighting; 5) Upper part of photo is an exterior door mat, shown with double doors in the open position. A custom rug inside echoes the pattern of the exterior mat.*

Cloisonné Mural: *This 10-foot high installation, shown with its original design drawing in the upper left image, is executed in hand-ground acrylic. It includes 72 level changes, 22 specially cut mirrors, and 2,000 feet of copper edging.*

154

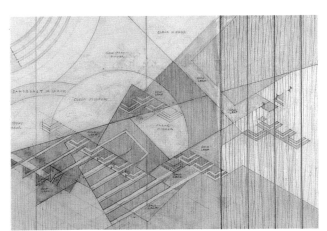

Art Glass, Mirrors, and Gold: *The mural at the top of the page combines mirrors with stained wood and gold leaf. In the center, a semi-circular skylight appears as a full circle by way of its mirrored reflection. To the right of the art glass skylight, the mirror is shown when it was masked and ready for sandblasting. The original sketch for the mural is shown directly above and the completed work appears to the right.*

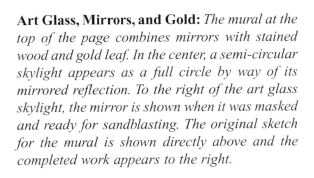

Desert Geology: *The top photo is a six-foot long mural, executed on seven levels, with oil paint, and silver and bronze leaf. It is an abstraction of the crystalline character of the desert land forms. The bottom left design is a geometric study which served as the basis for the custom entry door above. The sidelights are cast glass. The day lily mural on the facing page is shown together with a custom leather and wood table and custom bronze branch stand.*

C
ab
ve
ye
cl
ar

Vernon D. Garbrock 1998

Open yet Separate. *A single open space uses custom furnishings and a featured fireplace mass to create special areas for a sit-down bar to the left, the dining area in the foreground, the living room in the center, and a raised study and media area beyond. The bar looks down to city lights, while the tall butt-glazed glass on the right opens out to a panoramic backdrop of mountains.*

Mural, Bowls, and Branches: *The mural is an abstraction of the long sweeping curves of the desert agave plant. The multi-level piece mixes painted surfaces with silver and golf leaf. The black-plated steel bowls and branch stand are all custom designed as are the leather runners.*

The Magic of Glass: *From the table top and mitered glass on the facing page to the above applications of butt-glazing, light wells, frameless doors, horizontal mitered bands, and etched-glazing, glass is the material of mystery. Being invisible, its essence is its absence.*

Garden ornaments: *In the above photo, water flows through a bank of flowers into a pool. To the right a Soleri wind bell, suspended from a cantileved beam, mingles with blossoms below.*

Gardens, Water, and Fire

Like our planetary home, our bodies are comprised mainly of water and life cannot exist without it. The water that shimmers to delight our senses is the same water that carved the earth to create the Grand Canyon. Painters and poets have long referred to water as a powerful symbol of life and in the design of our homes, it should be used accordingly.

Walls, moats, and other structures once used for defense are now used for sensory delight. The most naturally beautiful homes are those that blur the distinction between their interiors and outside space. Transitional features used to extend interior space include outdoor living rooms, porches, terraces, balconies, pergolas, and garden walls.

Swimming pools can be designed as multipurpose reflecting ponds. Fountains can provide not only visual play, but a cooling effect from the sounds of splashing jets and cascades. Pools and fountains can be used to start the sense of arrival long before reaching the front door. Like outstretched arms, covered walkways, landscaped courtyards, and cascading streams and fountains can be used to create a bond between all structures and their natural settings.

Custom Steel Urn: *Fire shoots upward out of a bed of lava rocks while reflecting downward into the pool. The tree to the right grows out of a sunken island rimmed by a circular pool.*

165

Intimacy and Infinity: *The design of this pool and spa provides a sheltering sense of enclosure while remaining open to the horizon. Steps up to the spa, shown to the right, are separated by the greenery and aroma of growing mint. Instead of being utilitarian in appearance, swimming pools are most lovely when treated as cascades, streams, and reflecting ponds. By way of a dark bottom and careful treatment of the edge conditions, even a modest-size pool, can take on the character of a small lake as shown on the facing page.*

Primitive Sensations: *When combined with water, nothing so connects us with the mystery of creation as the dynamic character of fire. The powerful symbol of lashing flames has been with us since Prometheus first brought fire to the earth for human use. We may no longer depend on fires in the landscape to prepare food, but we covet this ancient symbol as a bridge between the primitive and our own creative spirit.*

Curving Water: *Broad sweeping arcs bring water directly to the edge of multi-level terraces. Being neither earth nor atmosphere, water is an embrace between the two. It can be silent, formless, and colorless, or it can come alive with continually changing sounds, formations, and a sparkling rainbow of colors. The gift of water is that we are delighted by its sights, sounds, and touch.*

Blending into the Natural: *Water cascades over huge rock forms before flowing under a walkway bridge and into the pool at the base of the spa. Stone walls and multi-level terraces weave in and around their natural setting.*

171

Reflecting Ponds: *Both of these fully functioning swimming pools have been designed as garden ponds. The pool on the facing page has a series of rock-ledge terraces for informal seating. In the above photo, a cascading water-wall flows into the pond which in turn flows over a negative edge, shielded by planting.*

Watery surprises: *The use of water is most rewarding when surrounded with lush vegetation and shady places. Imagination and playfulness are key. On the facing page, the richness of water and greenery is epitomized by the Patio de los Cipreses at the Generalife outside the Alhambra in Spain.*

To build with grandeur and purpose is to take a positive hand in creation

"First we shape our environments,
then they shape us."
– Winston Churchill

The Power of Heritage

The most exciting designs include a playful sense of discovery resulting from solutions that go well beyond the obvious. When "home" consists of multiple structures, the element of surprise can be heightened by a pleasant interplay between indoor and outdoor space. New forms of multi-building compounds, once the norm of family ranches, farms, and plantations, are reappearing in fresh form, offering both greater privacy as well as an opportunity for multi-generational, life-long environments.

Family Compounds

When the settings for more than one home can be considered as part of an overall plan, it is possible to design for the enhanced advantages of scale, shared driveways, shared gardens, and shared pools and spas. But the far greater advantages are all richly emotional. The custom compound is a place for a family to call home, not just for the moment but in a way that provides for the future. There is growing awareness that this sense of belonging is one of the greatest luxuries a family can provide for itself, and for generations to come.

Heritage compounds are a commitment to both family and place, something not everyone is able to make, but for those who can, the payoff is enormous. Whether or not your children and grandchildren come "home" is often a matter of whether or not they feel there is an inviting place to which they can return. Making that a special reality can be as sustaining to one's multi-generational well-being as any other form of estate planning for the future.

The drawings on the following four pages illustrate a "family triptych," — a three part work of art — designed to provide a home base for two, three, or four generations in a single setting, offering both uncommon convenience and independence for everyone involved. For some, the idea of a family compound may work best for seasonal use, and for others, as their primary home.

"A home is not a mere

transient shelter;

its essence

lies in its permanence ...

in its quality of representing,

in all its details, the

personalities of the people

who live in it."

– H.L. Mencken

Family Triptych: *Three residences, each complete in themselves, are made more rewarding by the shared amenities and presence of the others. The experience is very much like living with the amenities and atmosphere of a resort. When you step out of your own house, everything about the surrounding environment is yours to enjoy as well.*

"Beauty is the adjustment of all parts proportionately so that one cannot add or subtract or change without impairing the harmony of the whole."
– Leon Battista Alberti

Monticello

The author of our Declaration of Independence was also a celebrant of art and architecture. Thomas Jefferson's writings and life were one in the same. He crafted words to extol the sovereignty of the individual while his design of Monticello created the setting for civilized elegance. Both his words and his designs epitomized the quality of human dignity.

Like Mt. Vernon, Jefferson's design of Monticello is far more a genuine feature of its setting than anything to do with the pretense of crystal chandeliers or other extravagances of the past. Monticello is more inventive, even experimental, including 40 years of changes, as Jefferson pursued his passion for design.

"Every spirit builds itself a house,

and beyond its house a world,

and beyond its world,

a heaven.

Know then

That the world exists for you.

Build therefore, your own world."

– Ralph Waldo Emerson

◆

"Creativity is not merely

the innocent spontaneity of

our youth and childhood: it must

also be married to the passion of

the adult human being, which is a

passion to live

beyond one's death."

– Rollo May

Taliesin and Taliesin West

Frank Lloyd Wright's summer home consisted of 5,000 acres where central Wisconsin is most lovely. For the winter months, his home, Taliesin West included 1,200 acres at the base of Scottsdale's McDowell mountains.

In both locations, Wright was surrounded by his collection of museum-quality artwork, pottery, sculpture, and Japanese screens. Pools, fountains, and gardens were everywhere, including gardens for cutting flowers and those that provided fresh produce for his table. Many people are now beginning to enjoy media rooms or home theaters, but each of Wright's three theaters had fixed seating for over 100 people who routinely enjoyed first-run movies, dramatic performances, and live concerts.

He had daily dialogue with intelligent people from as many as 25 nations at any one time. Wright's efficient and supportive live/work environments were a significant factor in permitting him to enjoy his most productive years right up to his death just short of his 92nd birthday. He could conduct daily affairs without the hassle of commuting or traffic jams yet he loved cars, including his customized Lincoln Cabriolet, Cord, Mercedes Benz, and Bently. While Wright's homes cost money, how he lived was far more a matter of creative design and commitment than anything afforded by financial wealth alone.

Nothing is more powerful for creating heritage than the imaginative use and stewardship of land. Building grandly is the American replacement for the inherited aristocracies of the past.

Taliesin West: *Beyond its dramatic appearance lies a profound study of elements, all related to creating the truly custom home. Taliesin West is not only an uncommon exploration of structure, materials, light and space, but it is also one of the world's most elaborate examples of an integrated environment for life and work.*

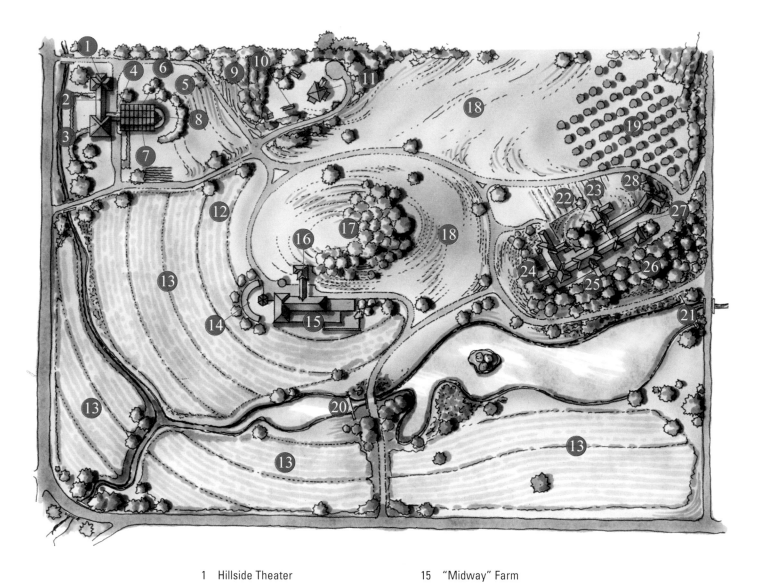

1	Hillside Theater	15	"Midway" Farm
2	Staff Dining	16	Staff Residence
3	Kitchen/Living Room above	17	Midway Hill
4	Bridge	18	Pasture
5	Drafting Room	19	Orchard
6	Staff Quarters	20	Upper Dam
7	Staff Quarters	21	Lower Dam
8	"Tea" Circle	22	Vineyard
9	Staff Residences	23	Hill Garden
10	Windmill: "Romeo & Juliet"	24	Main Residence
11	Tan-Y-Deri Residence	25	Studio
12	Vegetable Gardens	26	Lower Court
13	Cultivated Fields	27	Upper Court
14	Machinery Shed	28	Staff Residences

Taliesin in Wisconsin: *The above plan shows the three main groupings of buildings, "Hillside" in the upper left, "Midway" in the center, and "Taliesin" itself on the right, facing out to ponds which flow into the Wisconsin River.*

Taliesin Aerial: *The above photo corresponds to numbers 22 to 28 on the facing page. The Taliesin compound included Frank Lloyd Wright's home and studio, as well as offices, shops, and living quarters for his apprentices.*

At Home with Nature: *Frank Lloyd Wright's Wisconsin home was both a place of his personal explorations as well as a clear expression of his philosophy. He would say, "What is natural is not necessarily architectural, but what is architectural must always be natural." Taliesin is as much at home in its hillside setting as are its embracing stand of trees.*

The Town Ranch

Every home in this book is a modern day version of Mt. Vernon, Monticello, Taliesin, and Taliesin West, because they were each shaped by and for the life patterns of their owners. What distinguishes Washington, Jefferson, and Wright is the elaborate extent to which they tied their heritage to what they built on the land. Their homes provide beautiful, high-performance expressions of both their values and commitments.

In like manner, the Town Ranch idea is a highly personal place that can have as many versions as there are individuals with large-scale dreams and abilities.

The above plan includes 12 major land uses as listed on the facing page. "The Hacienda" is the main house complete with pools, fountains, shaded arcades, and vegetable and flower gardens. Its "pinwheel" design includes the master suite, a children's wing, service wing, and a wing for vehicles. All shared living spaces occur in the center.

The grounds include tennis courts, a golf putting course, citrus groves, and community-wide paths and trails. Five guest houses can be occupied as independent homes, each with its own guest suite. A planetarium is surrounded by a garden maze.

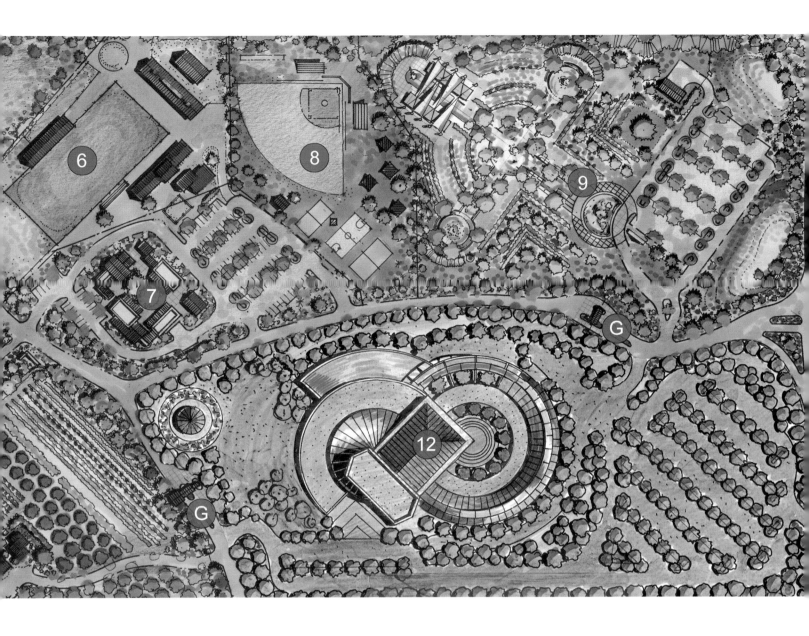

Opposite the entry to the main house is "The Town Square" with its personal pub, ice-cream parlor, post office, cinema, music pavilion, and hobby-related shops and studios. Flanking the Town Square are the stables, dressage arena, and a five-acre park. Adjacent to the park is a 15-acre botanical garden. A pair of gatehouses separates the circulation for a private school from the rest of the ranch.

The Town Ranch idea is one of creating a live/work environment with amenities that reinforce the dreams of imaginative people, including possibilities for everything from family gatherings to corporate retreats.

1. The Hacienda Main House
2. Tennis Courts, Barbeque, and Play Area
3. 18-hole Putting Course
4. Fresh Flowers and Produce
5. Individual Family or Guest Houses
6. Stables and Arena
7. Village Cinema, Music Pavilion, and Workshops
8. Five-Acre Park
9. Botanical Garden
10. Observatory
11. Garden Maze
12. Private School
G. Gated Entries

19 What if a separate interior designer and the architect don't get along?

A similar question could be asked concerning other members of the team. The finest professionals are accustomed to being challenged by each other, all to the betterment of the work. Select your team wisely and more likely than not, everyone will make it to the finish line with mutual and greater respect than when they started. In the rare instance where someone is not up to the challenge, they should be replaced.

20 How important is it to work with a local architect?

If you can find what you want close at hand, stick with a local team. If that is not possible, your design architect can be located anywhere you are willing to visit. During construction, your architect will come to the construction site on an as-needed basis. For all other times, a local representative will be on-site to observe the work. By way of telephone, facsimile, and email, the local representative serves as the architect's eyes and ears.

21 How much time will we need to spend with our architect?

This answer has two parts. Part one is the time your architect will require to fully understand how to give you his or her best. An equal or greater amount of time will go into helping you explore whatever possibilities you may want to consider in order to be certain of your judgments. During the construction phase, some clients attend a weekly meeting on-site with the architect and contractor, and others visit only occasionally, preferring to be kept informed with progress photos and minutes of all meetings.

22 Does the architect pick the general contractor?

In spite of repeated relationships with excellent builders, our preference is to start fresh each time with a selection process involving three or more contractors, all of whom are capable of doing the work. The first reason for this approach is that all contractors' workloads and personnel change over time. The second reason is that both the house and the client will have their own characteristics, which need to be matched with the most appropriate builder. We place extreme importance on this matter because selecting the right contractor is one of the most critical choices you will make.

23 What is meant by "Great buildings are only possible with great clients"?

The "great client" approaches the uncertainties of exploratory design, not as hardship, but as one of life's greatest luxuries. They can be challenging and exacting in their demands, but along with high expectations, great clients are a source of high inspiration, a joy to serve. It takes little effort to be supportive when everything is routinely falling into place. The great client is supportive when problems occur, recognizing that it is at such moments, that everyone is called upon to give their absolute best. Frank Lloyd Wright called it, "snatching victory from the jaws of defeat."

24 Is having a custom home worth the effort?

The answer can only be personal, just as it is for all individuals who pursue dreams that others do not have. Some dreams are easy to quantify, like winning a race, others are more difficult to describe, like the desire to live with beauty and authenticity. If something in you can be excited by the opportunity to shape your own environment, it is unlikely that you will be satisfied any other way. To build with artful integrity is to pursue dreams and desires that express and expand those special qualities that make you who you are.

The Language of Design

The following definitions of words and phrases are encountered during the process of design. This is not a listing of the component parts of architecture but rather the qualitative references and objectives relating to the custom home.

Ancestral Home: Typically thought of as something inherited from the past, but it can also be created in the future. By way of self-exploration and design, it is legitimately possible to dream of returning to an ancestral home that is yet to be.

Aristocracy: In the words of Frank Lloyd Wright, "Democracy is the greatest and highest form of aristocracy the world has ever seen, because it is aristocracy innate."

Authentic Design: Growing out of self-discovery, self-trust, without imitation, and employing an honest use of materials.

Bounced Light: Eliminating glare from direct sunlight, by deflecting light off the surrounds of deeply recessed windows, light shelves, or broad overhanging eaves.

Building Massing: Articulation of major and minor forms, including all exterior walls and roofs.

Character: Like a person who knows his or her own mind, a sure-footed sense that the design of the house represents a clarity of intention that made it to the finish line. The opposite of a design that feels confusing or uncertain of itself, with a little of this and a little of that.

Co-Creators: Architect and client working together on a path of mutual exploration and discovery.

Compound: Elements of home, decentralized in such a manner as to create connecting courtyards and other open space weaving between and around all living areas.

Context: The environs are to a house what a beautiful setting is to a jewel. The setting of a house includes site planning that acknowledges neighboring houses (existing or future), and the use of entry monuments, garden walls, landscaping, and lighting.

Custom Home: Not defined by size or cost, but by a shared commitment of Owner and Architect to reach beyond the short-cut of imitation.

Design: A conceptualizing, clarifying, and shaping that never stops. All phases of the work, including Schematic Design, Design Development, Construction Documents, and Construction Administration are centered on design. Each step represents an opportunity to reinforce the original concept by refining its details.

Dramatizing Space: Like the diminuendos and crescendos in music, the throttling down and opening up of entries and passageways to create contrast and spatial interest.

Environmentalist: While too-seldom the case, the true environmentalist cares as much about the quality of the built environment as he or she does about nature itself.

Exploratory Design: The architectural equivalent to the composer's sense of music yet unborn.

Flow: A spatial quality where architectural features define otherwise open, connected space, rather than resorting to separate rooms.

Grammar: Artful, consistent relationships. Just as abiding by the rules of language is helpful in being understood, for design to be understood as a work of art requires a coherent direction that establishes and abides by its own rules.

Heritage: Status or lot acquired not by inheritance, but through the designing spirit of energy, industry, and creativity.

Home: The unifying setting for whatever individual spaces are required to support the life of its occupants in optimal ways. This can be anything from a centralized structure to a series of decentralized spaces arranged more like a personal compound or village.

Indigenous: Growing out of a specific place and time. An authentic expression—a sense of belonging, as opposed to superimposing the characteristics of one place on another.

Integral Ornamentation: Murals, sculpture, wall hangings, carpets, leaded glass, and other features, designed to relate to the character of the house for which it is intended.

Integrity: Design that demonstrates a clear direction and stays true to itself from the largest to the smallest considerations.

Interior Design: Best when treated as a continuation of the architectural idea applied to all details of human use and comfort.

Livable Area: Enclosed space measured to the outside of the outside walls, excluding garage, garage storage, and mechanical equipment rooms.

Modulated Light: Between being outside in the direct sun and inside under roof, the intermediate use of canopies and trellises to transition from one quality and intensity of light to another.

Mystery: Not a problem to be solved but a beyond-the-obvious quality to be celebrated. Something that engages and inspires our deeper appreciation for things simple and complex at the same time.

Natural: Rather than referring to the birds and the bees, the word is most useful as an achievement of the spirit. The finest architecture is as natural as nature itself. It is humanity taking a positive hand in creation.

Nature of Materials: Not just the obvious differences but the inherent spiritual quality that distinguishes one material from another.

Organic: The living systems of nature in which the smallest part relates to the totality, like the cellular structure of our bodies, in which each cell carries with it the coding for the entire system.

Ellis, Estelle, Seebohm, Caroline, & Sykes, Christopher. *At Home with Books*, New York: Carol Southern Books, 1995

Fields, Rick. *Chop Wood Carry Water*, Los Angeles: Tarcher, 1984

Garrett, Wendell. *George Washington's Mount Vernon*, New York: The Monacelli Press, Inc., 1998

Gilliatt, Mary. *Dream Houses*, Boston: Little, Brown and Company, 1987

Glancey, Jonathan & Richard Bryant. *The New Moderns*, San Francisco: Soma Books, 1990

Grudin, Robert. *Time and the Art of Living*, New York: Harper & Row Publishers, 1982

Galfetti, Gustau Gili. *My House, My Paradise*, Corte Madera, California: Gingko Press, Inc., 1999

Hart, Spencer. *Wright Rooms*, New Jersey: Chartwell Books, 1998

Harwood, Barbara Bannon. *The Healing House*, Carlsbad, California: Hay House, Inc., 1997

Hildebrand, Grant. *Origins of Architectural Pleasure*, Berkeley and Los Angeles, California: University of California Press, 1999; London, England: University of California Press, Ltd., 1999

Jones, Jeremy. *Homes for Creative Living*, San Francisco: Chronicle Books, 1984

Katz, Peter. *The New Urbanism*, New York: McGraw-Hill, 1994

Kidder, Tracy. *House*, New York: Avon Books, 1985

Langdon, Philip. *American Houses*, New York: Stewart, Tabori & Chang, 1987

Lawlor, Anthony. *A Home for the Soul*, New York: Clarkson Potter, 1997

——————— *The Temple in the House*, New York, Tarcher, 1994

Lind, Carla. *The Wright Style*, New York: Simon & Schuster, 1992

Lloyd, Claire. *Sensual Living*, London: Conran Octopus Limited, 1998

Manroe, Candac Ord. *Uncluttered*, New York: Friedman/Fairfax Publishers, 1997

Marcus, Clare Cooper. *House as a Mirror of Self*, Berkeley, Conari Press, 1995

Marinelli, Janet with Kourik, Robert. *The Naturally Elegant Home*, Canada: Little, Brown & Co., 1992

Marinelli, Janet with Bierman-Lytle, Paul. *Your Natural Home*, New York: Little, Brown and Company, 1995

McMillian, Elizabeth. *Casa California, Spanish Style Houses from Santa Barbara to San Clemente*, New York: Rizolli International Publications, Inc., 1996

Moe, Richard & Wilke, Carter. *Changing Places*, New York: Henry Holt and Company, 1997

Moore, Charles W., Ruble, John, Yudell, Buzz. *Houses and Housing*, Massachusetts: Rockport Publishers, 1994

Moore, Charles, Allen, Gerald, & Lyndon, Donlyn. *The Place of Houses*, New York: Holte, Rinehart and Winston, 1974

Nelessen, Anton Clarence. *Visions for a New American Dream*, Chicago: American Planning Association, 1994

Oshima, Ken Tadashi and Kinoshita, Toshiko. *Visions of the Real: 11, Modern Houses in the 20th Century*, Architecture and Urbanism, October 2000

Pagram, Beverly. *Home & Heart*, Daybreak, 1998

Pearson, David. *The Natural House Book*, New York, Fireside, 1989

———————— *Earth to Spirit*, San Francisco: Chronicle Books, 1995

Pfeiffer, Bruce Brooks. *Frank Lloyd Wright: Selected Houses 2*, Tokyo: A.D.A. Edita, 1990

Post, Steven. *The Modern Book of Feng Shui*, New York: Dell Publishing, 1998

Riera Ojeda, Oscar. *The New American House 2*, New York: Whitney Library of Design, 1997

Rossbach, Sarah. *Interior Design with Feng Shui*, New York: Arkana, 1987

Rykwert, Joseph. *The Villa, Ancient to Modern*, New York: Harry N. Abrams, Inc. Publishers, 2000

Sagar, Louis. *Zona Home*, New York: Harper Collins Publishers, Inc. 1996

Smith, Kathryn. *Frank Lloyd Wright's Taliesin and Taliesin West*, New York: Harry N. Abrams, Inc. Publishers, 1997

Street-Porter, Tim. *Tropical Houses – Living in Nature in Jamaica, Sri Lanka, Java, Bali, and the Coasts of Mexico and Belize*, New York: Clarkson Potter/Publishers, 2000

Steele, James. *Sustainable Architecture: Principles, Paradigms and Case Studies*, New York: McGraw-Hill, 1997

Susanka, Sarah. *The Not So Big House*, Connecticut: Taunton Press, 1998

Swaback, Vernon D. *Designing the Future*, Tempe, Arizona: Herberger Center for Design Excellence, 1997

Tanizaki, Jun'ichiro. *In Praise of Shadows*, Connecticut: Leete's Island Books, 1977

Tatum, Rita. *The Alternative House*, Los Angeles: Reed Books, 1978

Too, Lillian. *The Complete Illustrated Guide to Feng Shui*, New York: Barnes & Noble, 1996

The Apprentice Years 1957–1959: *Clockwise from upper left, the author with Frank Lloyd Wright readying a model for a television appearance in Chicago; discussing a design at Taliesin West in Arizona; and, working in the drafting room at Taliesin in Wisconsin.*

About the Author

Vernon D. Swaback was born and raised in Chicago where he first felt the influence of Frank Lloyd Wright's houses in Oak Park and surrounding suburban areas. In 1957, he traveled to Arizona to become Wright's youngest apprentice, residing at Taliesin West during the winter months, and during the summers, at Taliesin in Wisconsin. He remained with the Wright organization for 22 years before founding an independent practice. He is now managing partner of *Studio V Interior Design* and *Swaback Partners*, a 40-person firm of architects and planners.

His prior writings include, *Production Dwellings, An Opportunity for Excellence*, published by the Wisconsin Department of Natural Resources, and *Designing the Future*, published by the College of Architecture and Environmental Design at Arizona State University. The author/architect resides with his wife and two daughters in Scottsdale, Arizona.

"You are a king

by your own fireside,

as much as

any monarch, on his throne."

– Cervantes

THE JOY OF DESIGN.
WHAT BEGINS
AS A RELATIONSHIP
BETWEEN ARCHITECT AND CLIENT
ULTIMATELY CREATES
OUR WORLD OF
FORM, COLOR, SPACE,
AND THE
TOTAL ENVIRONMENT